VOGUE® KNITTING

Mittens & Gloves

VOGUE® KNITTING

Mittens & Gloves

the editors of Vogue Knitting Magazine

Sixth&Spring Books
161 Avenue of the Americas
New York, NY 10013

PHOTO CREDITS:
Paul Amato for LVARepresents.com: pp. 2, 5 (top, second from bottom), 10, 12, 13, 14, 17, 21, 24, 26, 32, 36, 38, 40, 42, 46, 57, 58, 62, 66, 82, 85, 88, 91, 92, 94, 97, 102, 107, 123, 124

Rose Callahan: 5 (second from top, bottom), 6, 9, 18, 20, 72, 74, 75, 76, 78, 81, 98, 100, 108, 110, 111, 112, 119, 126, 128, 130, 136

Carlo Dalla Chiesa: p. 52

Patrick Demarchelier: p. 71

Jack Deutsch: p. 34

Haitem: p. 115

Jim Jordan for JimJordanPhotography.com: pp. 101, 120

Rudy Molacek: p. 104

Marcus Tullis: pp. 47, 132, 135

Marco Zambelli: pp. 48, 116

Some of the yarns used for the projects shown may have been discontinued. To find a suitable substitute yarn, be sure to knit a gauge swatch to obtain the correct finished measurements. Take care that both the stitch and row gauge match those listed in the pattern instructions and TAKE TIME TO CHECK GAUGES. Also note that yarn amounts may vary depending on the weight and yardage of the substitute yarn.

Library of Congress Control Number: 2010926070
ISBN: 978-1-936096-05-3

Manufactured in China
1 3 5 7 9 10 8 6 4 2

Contents

p. 10

p. 78

p. 107

p. 136

Warm Hands Warm Heart

When we looked into our archives for our favorite mitten and glove patterns from the issues of *Vogue Knitting* and *Knit.1* magazines, it truly warmed our hearts to find so many wonderful designs.

Not only were there plenty of traditional styles, including Fair Isle mittens and Aran gloves, but there were also contemporary and cutting-edge wristlets, fashion-forward gauntlets and fun-loving muffs. In short, something for everyone.

Mittens and gloves often get left behind in the world of cold-weather knitwear. Scarves are every beginner's favorite, and hats are perfect for a last-minute present, but no snowy day can be enjoyed without something to keep the fingers warm. I'm glad to report that, with *Vogue Knitting Mittens & Gloves*, hands finally get a leg up. We've handpicked—no pun intended—these patterns to help knitters of every level discover (or remember) the world of mittens and gloves. Fun and funky fingerless mitts are a perfect first project to get those dpns clicking, and novice knitters will soon learn that fingers aren't so scary after all. More advanced knitters will find a satisfying showcase for intricate colorwork, lace patterns and cables. And no need to leave hats and scarves out of the fun: Several of these delightful patterns come as part of a matching ensemble.

The innovative handwarmers in this collection cover more than twenty-five years of knitting expertise and represent some of the best designers out there. Many of the projects knit up quickly and with very little yarn to make great gifts for any occasion. With all the varied designs, you'll find something for everyone on your list, or just to complement every item in your own winter wardrobe. Perhaps you'll find yourself wishing you had more than two hands to keep warm—and to knit with, of course! We hope you enjoy creating these wonderful pieces as much as we've enjoyed rediscovering them.

Trisha Malcolm

Editor in Chief, *Vogue Knitting*

Smitten with

Mittens are hands down the best way to keep your paws toasty all winter long and are the perfect canvas for color and creativity.

Mittens

LET IT
SNOW

Snowbird Mittens

Use stranded colorwork to achieve the picturesque motifs central to Elli Stubenrauch's wintry mittens. They're perfect for your next snowball fight.

KNITTED MEASUREMENTS

Hand circumference 8¼"/21cm

Length from wrist to tip 9¾"/24.5cm

SIZE Sized for adult woman.

MATERIALS

1 1¾oz/50g hank (approx 185yd/169m) each of Louet North America *Gems Fingering* (superwash wool) in #54 teal (A) and #36 linen grey (B) (1)

Set of 5 size 1 (2.25mm) double-pointed needles (dpns) OR SIZE TO OBTAIN GAUGE

Stitch marker and scrap yarn

GAUGE

37 sts and 43 rnds = 4"/10cm over chart pat using size 1 (2.25mm) needles.

TAKE TIME TO CHECK GAUGE.

STITCH GLOSSARY

Kfb K into front and back of st—1 st inc'd.

M1R Insert LH needle from back to front under the strand between last st worked and next st on LH needle. K into front loop to twist the st.

M1L Insert LH needle from front to back under the strand between last st worked and next st on LH needle. K into back loop to twist the st.

CORRUGATED RIB (over a multiple of 3 sts)

Rnd 1 *With A, k1, bring B to front of work and p2, bring B to back; rep from * around.

Rep rnd 1 for corrugated rib.

LEFT MITTEN

Cuff With A, cast on 63 sts, divided over 4 dpns. Place marker (pm) and join, taking care not to twist sts. Work in corrugated rib for 1¾"/4.5cm.

Next (inc) rnd With A, *kfb, k5, kfb, k2, kfb, k5; rep from * 3 times more, end kfb, k2—76 sts. Cont in St st as foll:

Beg chart 1 Work rnds 1–3 of chart 1.

Thumb gusset

Rnd 4 With A, M1R, k1, M1L, work to end of rnd—78 sts. Cont to foll chart in this manner, working incs as shown, through chart rnd 32—106 sts.

Rnd 33 Work across first 30 sts for thumb, then place these sts on scrap yarn, work to end of rnd—76 sts. Cont to work to top of chart, working decs at top of mitten as shown—28 sts. With A, join 14 sts each side, using 3-needle bind-off (see page 144).

Thumb

Divide 30 sts on scrap yarn evenly over 3 dpns. Pm and join.

Beg chart 2

Work rnds 1–10 of chart 2, working decs and incs as shown on chart—30 sts.

Top shaping

Next (dec) rnd With A, [k2tog] 15 times—15 sts.

Next (dec) rnd With A, k1, [k2tog] 7 times—8 sts.

Cut A, leaving a 6"/15cm tail. Thread through rem sts and cinch tightly to close.

RIGHT MITTEN

Work as for left mitten, foll charts 3 and 4.

FINISHING

Sew gap between thumb and hand closed. ✣

CHART 1

CHART 2

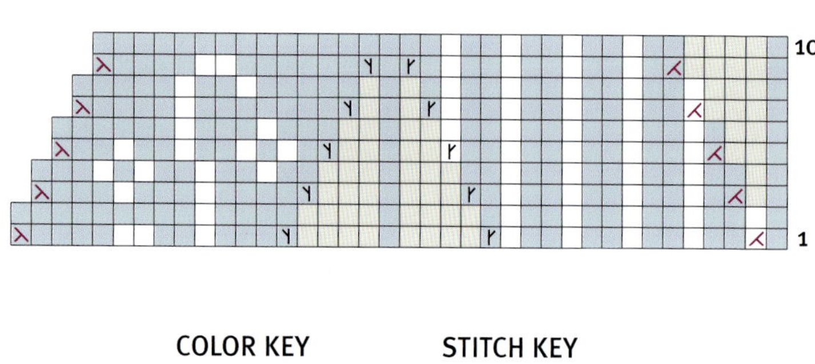

COLOR KEY

- Teal (A)
- Linen Grey (B)

STITCH KEY

- No stitch
- M1R
- M1L
- K2tog
- Ssk

CHART 3

74
70
60
50
40
30
20
10
1

76 sts

CHART 4

10
1

SNOW

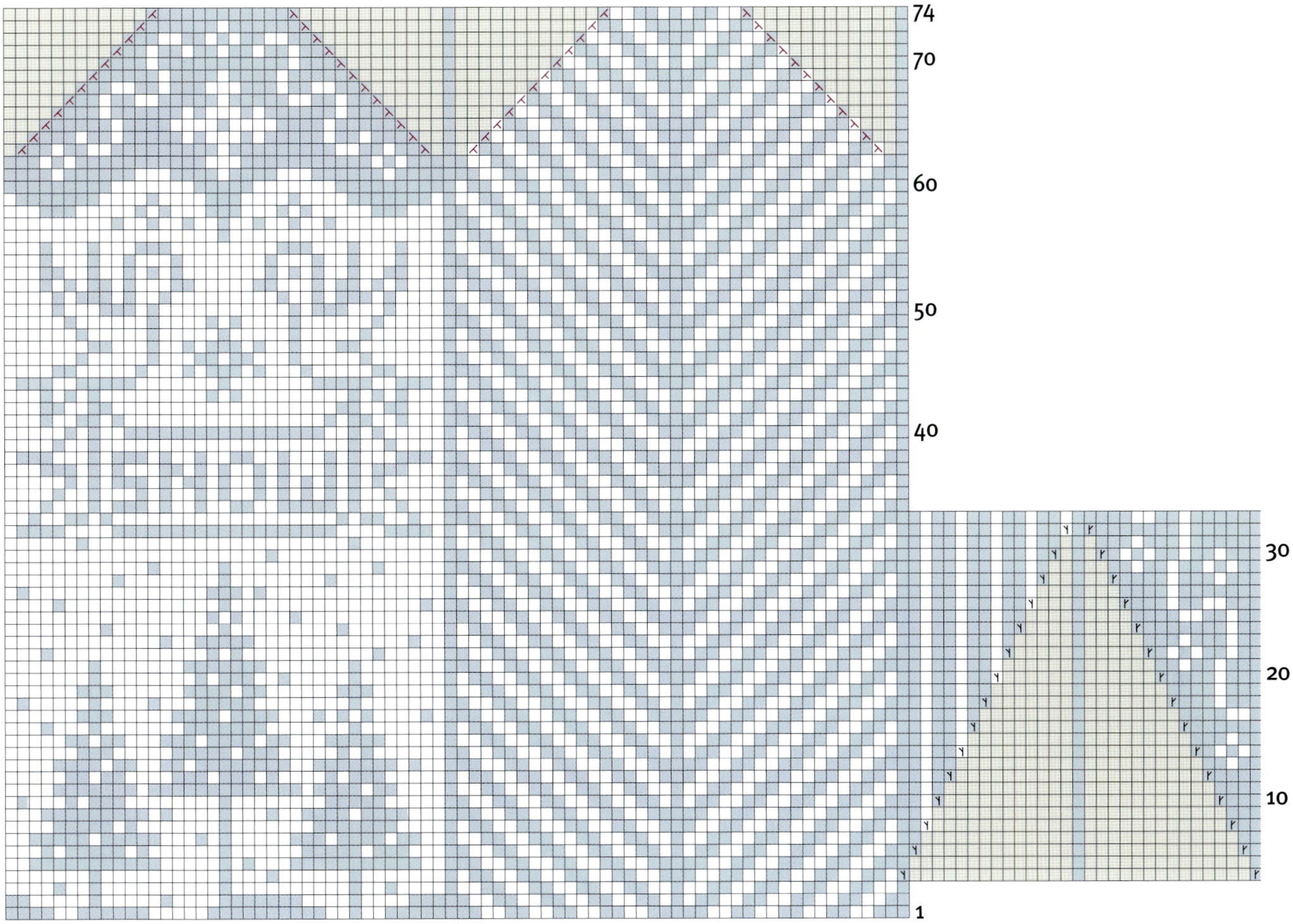

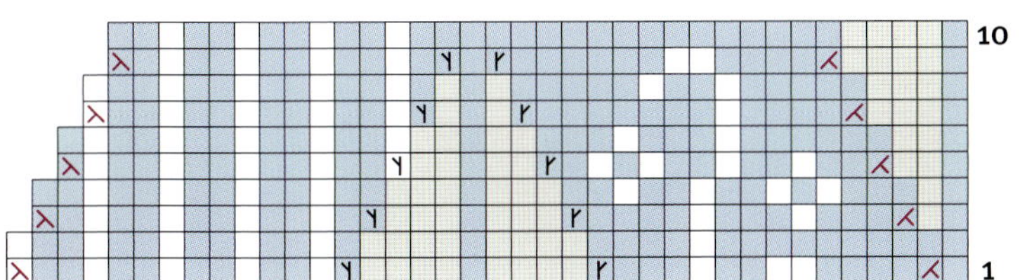

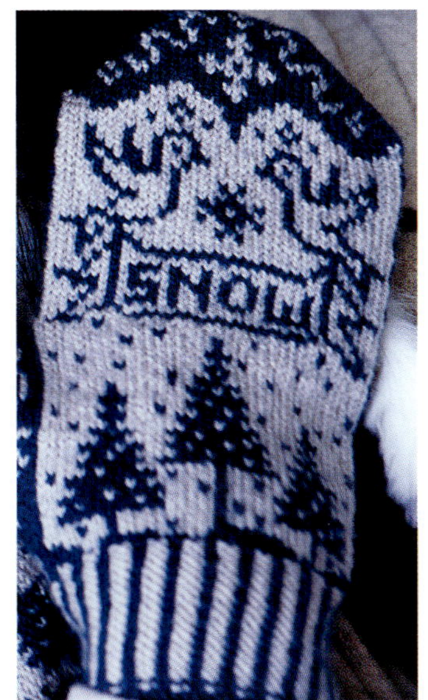

Trellis Mittens

These intricate mitts by Mari Muinonen are worked in a lattice cable pattern with whimsical bobble details. Knit in a warm shade of yellow, they'll add a touch of sun to a cloudy day.

KNITTED MEASUREMENTS

Hand circumference 7½"/19cm

Length of cuff 3½"/9cm

SIZE

One size.

MATERIALS

Original Yarn

2 3½oz/100g hanks (each approx 138yd/125m) of Manos del Uruguay/Fairmount Fibers, Ltd., *Handspun Semi Solids* (wool) in straw (4)

Substitute Yarn

2 3½oz/100g hanks (each approx 138yd/125m) of Manos del Uruguay/Fairmount Fibers, Ltd., *Wool Clasica* (wool) in z-straw (4)

Set of 4 size 8 (5mm) double-pointed needles (dpns) OR SIZE TO OBTAIN GAUGE

Cable needle (cn)

Stitch markers and scrap yarn

GAUGE

14 sts and 20 rnds = 4"/10cm over St st using size 8 (5mm) needles.

TAKE TIME TO CHECK GAUGE.

NOTE

For smaller-fitting mittens, use needles 1 size smaller than recommended needles.

STITCH GLOSSARY

3-st RC Sl 2 to cn, hold to *back,* k1, k2 from cn.

3-st LC Sl 1 to cn, hold to *front,* k2, k1 from cn.

3-st RPC Sl 2 to cn, hold to *back,* k1, p2 from cn.

3-st LPC Sl 1 to cn, hold to *front,* p2, k1 from cn.

4-st RC Sl 2 to cn, hold to *back,* k2, k2 from cn.

4-st LC Sl 2 to cn, hold to *front,* k2, k2 from cn.

4-st RPC Sl 2 to cn, hold to *back,* k2, p2 from cn.

4-st LPC Sl 2 to cn, hold to *front,* p2, k2 from cn.

Make Bobble (MB) [K1, p1] twice into 1 st, turn. P4, turn. [K2tog] twice, turn. P2tog, turn.

LEFT MITTEN

I-cord trim **(see page 145)**

Cast on 4 sts. Work I-cord as foll:

***Next row (RS)** With 2nd dpn, k4, do not turn. Slide sts back to beg of needle to work next row from RS; rep from * until 40 rows have been worked. Cut yarn, leaving an 18"/46cm tail, thread tail into tapestry needle. Graft ends tog to form a ring.

Cuff

Beg at grafted seam, pick up and k 1 st in each row around ring—40 sts, dividing sts over 3 needles as foll: 8 sts on first needle, 8 sts on 2nd needle (16 sts for palm side of hand) and 24 sts on 3rd needle (back of hand). Place marker (pm) for beg of rnd and join.

(**Note** At end of rnd 1/beg of rnd 2, work 4-st RC as foll: Sl last 2 sts of rnd 1 to cn and hold to back, remove rnd marker, k2, replace marker, k2 from cn.)

Beg chart 1

Work rnds 1–8 of chart 1 twice.

Thumb gusset

Beg chart 2

Inc rnd 1 K11, pm, M1, k2, M1, pm (thumb gusset), k3, work rnd 1 of chart 2 over 24 sts—42 sts.

Next 2 rnds K18, work chart 2 over 24 sts.

Inc rnd 2 K to first marker, sl marker, M1, k to 2nd marker, M1, sl marker, k3, work chart 2 over 24 sts—44 sts.

Next rnd K20, work chart 2 over 24 sts.

Next rnd Rep inc rnd 2—46 sts.

Next rnd K22, work chart 2 over 24 sts.

Next rnd Rep inc rnd 2—48 sts.

Next rnd K24, work chart 2 over 24 sts.

Next rnd K11, place 10 gusset sts on scrap yarn (removing markers), cast on 2 sts, k3, work chart 2 over 24 sts—40 sts divided over 3 needles as before: 8 sts each on first and 2nd needles, 24 sts on 3rd needle. Cont in pats as established through chart rnd 38 (removing and replacing rnd marker for cable on rnds 37 and 38 as before, because the 3-st LC and 3-st RC use 1 st from each side of the St st palm)—35 sts.

Next (dec) rnd K1, pm, ssk, k12, k2tog, pm, k1, ssk, p13, k2tog—31 sts.

Next (dec) rnd K1, sl marker, ssk, k to 2 sts before next marker, k2tog, sl marker, k1, ssk, p to last 2 sts of rnd, k2tog—27 sts. Rep the last rnd 4 times more—11 sts. Cut yarn, leaving a 6"/15cm tail. Thread through rem sts and cinch tightly to secure.

Thumb

Divide 10 thumb gusset sts over 2 needles.

Next rnd Join yarn and knit across sts, with 3rd needle pick up and k 4 sts along 2 cast-on sts—14 sts. Divide sts over 3 dpns. Join and pm for beg of rnds. Cont in St st for 13 rnds.

Top shaping

Dec rnd [K2tog] 7 times—7 sts.

Next rnd Knit.

Dec rnd [K2tog] 3 times, k1—4 sts. Cut yarn, leaving a 6"/15cm tail. Finish as for top of mitten.

RIGHT MITTEN

I-cord trim

Work as for left mitten.

Cuff

Pick up and k 40 sts as for left mitten, dividing sts over 3 needles as foll: 24 sts on first needle (back of hand), 8 sts on 2nd needle and 8 sts on 3rd needle (16 sts for palm side of hand). Pm for beg of rnd.

Beg chart 3

Work rnds 1–8 of chart 3 twice, working 4-st LC at end of rnd 1/beg of rnd 2 as foll: Sl 2 sts to cn and hold to front, remove marker, k2, replace marker, k2 from cn.

Thumb gusset

Beg chart 4

Inc rnd 1 Work rnd 1 of chart 4 over 24 sts, k3, pm, M1, k2, M1, pm (thumb gusset), k11—42 sts.

Next 2 rnds Work chart 4 over 24 sts, k18.

Inc rnd 2 Work chart 4 over 24 sts, k to first marker, sl marker, M1, k to 2nd marker, M1, sl marker, k11—44 sts.

Next rnd Work chart 4 over 24 sts, k20.

Next rnd Rep inc rnd 2—46 sts.

Next rnd Work chart 4 over 24 sts, k22.

Next rnd Rep inc rnd 2—48 sts.

Next rnd Work chart 4 over 24 sts, k24.

Next rnd Work chart 4 over 24 sts, k3, place 10 gusset sts on scrap yarn (removing markers), cast on 2 sts, k11—40 sts divided as before: 24 sts on first needle and 8 sts each on 2nd and 3rd needles.

Complete as for left mitten, following chart 4. ✢

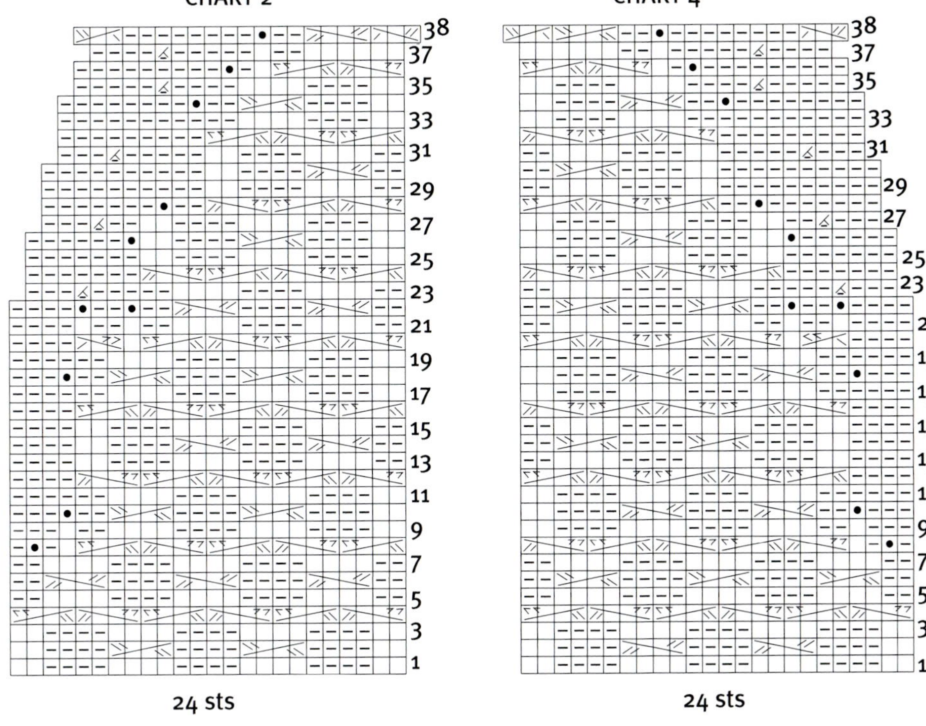

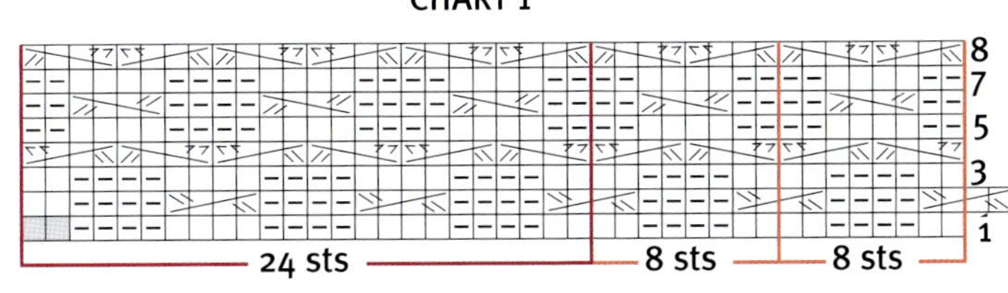

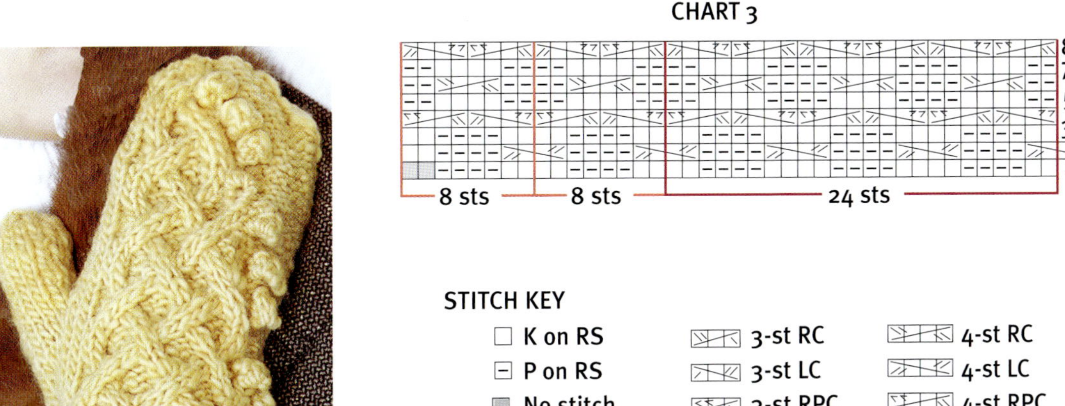

STITCH KEY

- K on RS
- P on RS
- No stitch
- Make bobble
- P2tog
- 3-st RC
- 3-st LC
- 3-st RPC
- 3-st LPC
- 4-st RC
- 4-st LC
- 4-st RPC
- 4-st LPC

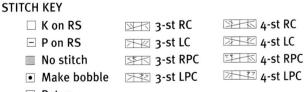

Striped Mittens

These exuberantly colorful oversized mittens by Tanis Gray will be the focal point of any cold-weather outfit. Braided drawstrings with colorful pom-poms complete the look.

KNITTED MEASUREMENTS

Hand circumference 8"/20.5cm

Length 9½"/24cm

SIZE

Sized for adult woman.

MATERIALS

1 3½oz/100g hank (approx 145yd/133m) each of Aslan Trends *Guanaco* (alpaca/wool) in #63 wonder (A), #46 blue jeans (B), #22 chocolate (C), #37 bone (D), #30 blush (E), #172 pomegranate (F) and #52 papaya (G) (5)

Set of 4 each sizes 8 and 10 (5 and 6mm) double-pointed needles (dpns) OR SIZE TO OBTAIN GAUGE

Crochet hook

Scrap yarn

2"/5cm pom-pom maker

Tapestry needle

Stitch marker and holders

GAUGE

15 sts and 18 rnds = 4"/10cm over St st using larger needles.

TAKE TIME TO CHECK GAUGE.

PROVISIONAL CAST-ON

Using scrap yarn and crochet hook, ch the number of cast-on sts, plus a few extra. Cut yarn and pull the tail through the last chain to secure. With knitting needle and yarn, pick up the required number of cast-on sts through the "purl bumps" on the back of the chain. Be careful not to split the waste yarn, as this makes it difficult to pull out the chain at the end. When it's time to remove the chain, pull out the tail from the last ch st. Gently and slowly pull on the tail to unravel the crochet stitches, carefully placing each released knit st on a needle as you go.

LEFT MITTEN

With A, cast on 30 sts, using provisional cast-on. Divide sts evenly over 3 larger dpns. Place marker (pm), and join.

Picot edging

Rnds 1–3 Knit.

Rnd 4 (eyelet rnd) *Yo, k2tog; rep from * around.

Rnds 5–7 Knit.

Join hem Place cast-on sts onto smaller dpns (removing chain). Fold hem to WS at eyelet rnd so that needles are tog. Join as foll: *Insert RH needle into 1 st on front needle and 1 cast-on st and k these 2 sts tog; rep from * around.

Beg chart

Work chart rnds 1–16.

Thumb placement

Rnd 17 With A, k14, place last 6 sts knit on a holder, k to end of rnd.

Next rnd With A, k to thumb placement, cast on 6 sts, k to end of rnd. Work through chart rnd 34.

Top shaping

Rnd 35 (dec rnd) [Ssk, k11, k2tog] twice—26 sts.

Cont to work 4 decs every rnd 5 times more—6 sts. Cut yarn and thread tail through rem sts. Pull tightly to close.

Thumb

With A, place 6 thumb sts onto larger dpn. Pick up and k8 sts around thumb opening, distribute over 4 dpns—14 sts. K every rnd in the foll color sequence: 1 rnd A, 1 rnd D, 2 rnds E, 1 rnd D, 1 rnd C, 1 rnd G, 2 rnds D, 2 rnds F.

Next rnd With F, [k2tog] 7 times—7 sts. Break yarn, thread tail through rem sts and pull tightly to close.

Cord and pom-poms

Cut six 48"/122cm strands of D. Holding 2 strands tog, braid a 30"/76cm cord. Weave cord through eyelet rnd, tie in bow. Using A, C and D, make four 2"/5cm pom-poms and secure to ends of cords.

RIGHT MITTEN

Work as for left mitten, except work thumb placement as foll:

Rnd 17 K22 with A, place last 6 sts just knit on a holder, k to end of rnd. ✣

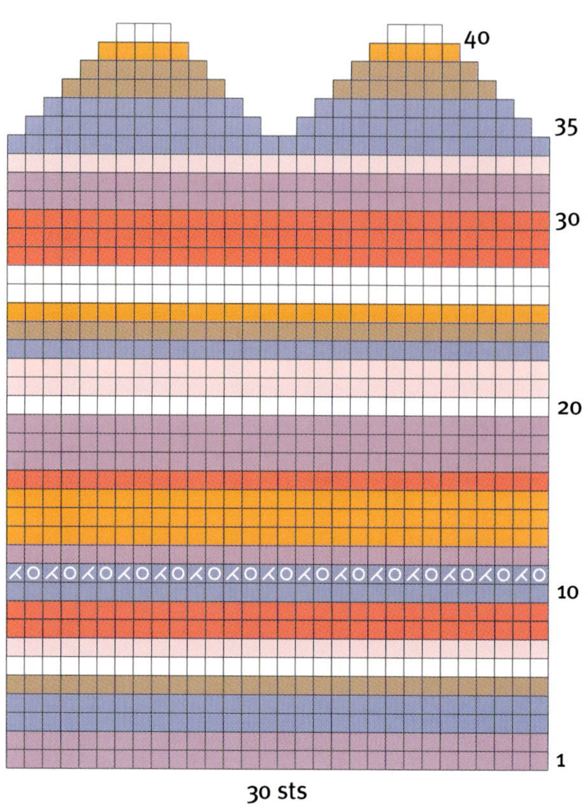

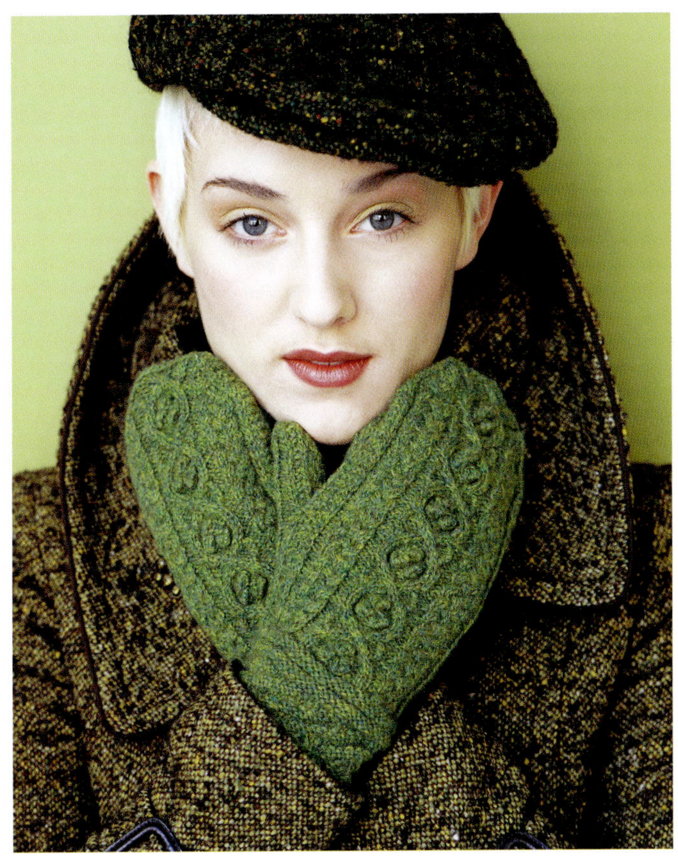

Multipattern Tweed Mittens

It's a festival of textures with Jared Flood's surprisingly understated mittens: Cables, bobbles, a slip-stitch palm and a chevron-stitch cuff work together in delightful harmony.

KNITTED MEASUREMENTS

Hand circumference 7½"/19cm

Length of cuff 3"/7.5cm

SIZE

Sized for adult woman.

MATERIALS

3 .88oz/25g balls (each approx 115yd/105m) of Jamieson's/Simply Shetland *2-Ply Spindrift* (shetland wool) in #259 leprechaun (1)

Set of 5 size 3 (3.25mm) double-pointed needles (dpns) OR SIZE TO OBTAIN GAUGE

Cable needle (cn)

Stitch markers and scrap yarn

GAUGE

32 sts and 40 rnds = 4"/10cm over St st using size 3 (3.25mm) needles.

TAKE TIME TO CHECK GAUGE.

STITCH GLOSSARY

2-st RPC Sl 1 to cn, hold to *back*, k1 tbl, p1 from cn.

2-st LPC Sl 1 to cn, hold to *front*, p1, k1 tbl from cn.

4-st RC Sl 2 to cn, hold to *back*, k2, k2 from cn.

4-st LC Sl 2 to cn, hold to *front*, k2, k2 from cn.

4-st RPC Sl 2 to cn, hold to *back*, k2, p2 from cn.

4-st LPC Sl 2 to cn, hold to *front*, k2, p2 from cn.

5-st LPC Sl 2 to cn, hold to *front*, k2, p1, then k2 from cn.

Make Bobble (MB) [K1, p1, k1, p1, k1] in same st—5 sts; then pass the 4th, 3rd, 2nd and first sts, one at a time, over the last st made.

LEFT MITTEN

Cuff

Cast on 54 sts, divided evenly over 4 dpns. Place marker (pm) and join, taking care not to twist sts.

Beg chart 1

Rnd 1 Work 6-st rep of chart 9 times. Cont to work through chart rnd 37.

Next rnd Knit.

Next (inc) rnd Sl 1 wyib, p3, sl 1 wyib, [M1, k4] 7 times, M1, k1, sl 1 wyib, p3, sl 1 wyib, [M1, k3] 4 times, M1, k2, sl 1 wyib, M1—68 sts.

Beg chart 2

Beg and end as indicated for left mitten, work rnds 1–26 of chart 2.

Rnd 27 Work to last 12 sts, place these 12 sts on scrap yarn for thumb, cast on 10 sts—66 sts. Join and cont to work through rnd 81—40 sts.

Saddle closing

Divide sts over needles as foll: first 5 sts on first needle (saddle), next 15 sts on 2nd needle (backside), next 5 sts on scrap yarn (saddle), last 15 sts on 3rd needle (palmside). Work back and forth over the 5 sts of saddle using a 4th needle as foll:

Row 1 (RS) Sl first st, p3, ssk last st tog with next st on 2nd needle; turn.

Row 2 Sl first st, p3, purl tog last st with next st on 3rd needle; turn. Rep these 2 rows, dec 1 st from either front or back of mitten at end of each row until all sts on needles 2 and 3 have been used—10 sts. Place sts on scrap yarn onto dpn and bind off saddles using 3-needle bind-off (see page 144).

Thumb

Beg at outer edge of palm, pick up and k12 sts along 10 cast-on sts as foll: K into front and back of first st to pick up 2 sts, pick up 1 in each of next 8 sts, k into front and back of last st to pick up 2 sts, pm for beg of rnd, sl 12 sts from scrap yarn to 2 more dpns, divide for 8 sts on each dpn. Join to work in rnds.

Beg chart 3

Work rnds 1–33 of chart—12 sts.

Next (dec) rnd [K2tog] 6 times—6 sts. Cut yarn leaving a 6"/15cm tail. Thread through rem sts and cinch tightly to close.

RIGHT MITTEN

Cuff

Cast on and work chart 1 as for left mitten through rnd 37.

Next rnd Knit.

Next (inc) rnd M1, sl 1 wyib, k1, [M1, k3] 4 times, M1, k1, sl 1 wyib, p3, sl 1 wyib, [M1, k4] 7 times, M1, k1, sl 1 wyib, p3, sl 1 wyib—68 sts.

Beg chart 2

Beg and end as indicated for right mitten, work rnds 1–26 of chart 2.

Rnd 27 Sl first 12 sts to scrap yarn, cast on 10 sts, work to end—66 sts. Work through rnd 81—40 sts.

Saddle closing

Divide sts over needles as foll: first 15 sts on first needle (palmside), next 5 sts on 2nd needle (saddle), next 15 sts on 3rd needle (backside), last 5 sts on scrap yarn (saddle).

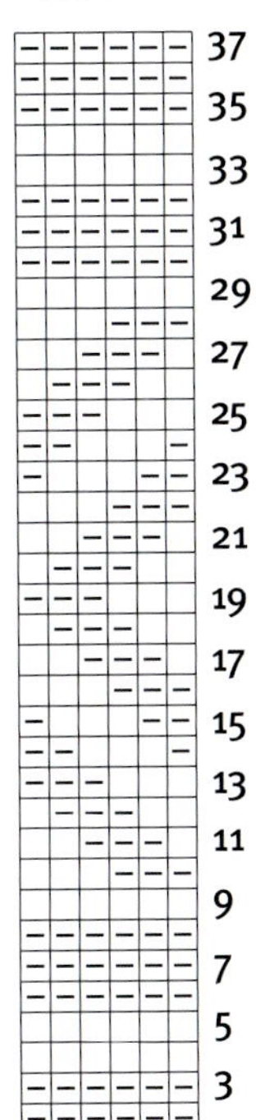

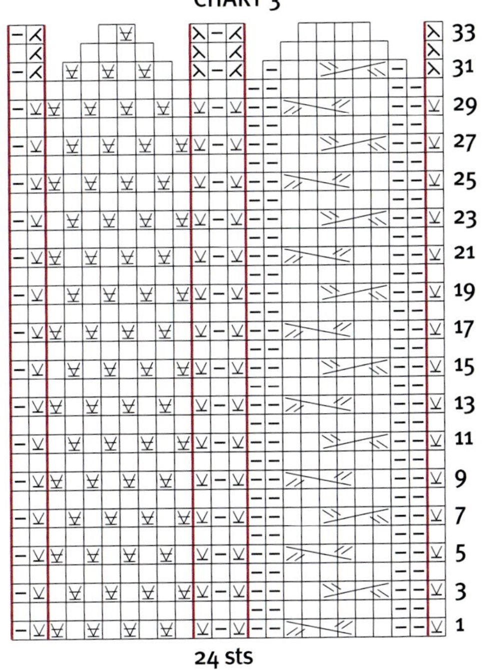

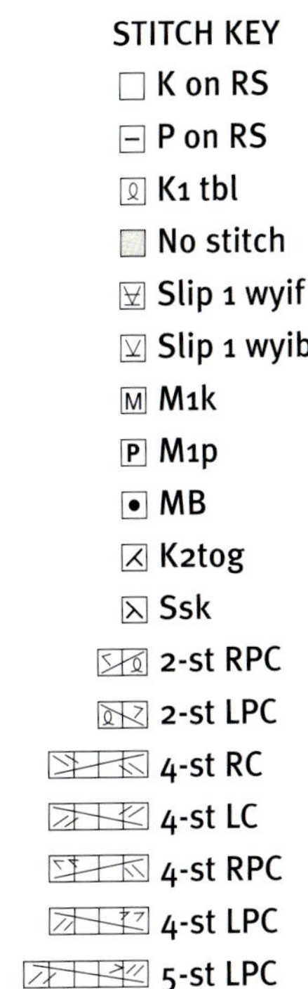

Join yarn to work back and forth over the 5 sts of the saddle using a 4th needle as foll:

Row 1 (RS) Sl first st, p3, ssk last st tog with next st on 3rd needle; turn.

Row 2 Sl first st, p3, purl tog last st with next st on first needle; turn. Rep these 2 rows, dec 1 st from either front or back of mitten at end of each row until all sts on needles 2 and 3 have been used—10 sts. Place sts on scrap yarn onto dpn and bind-off saddles using 3-needle bind-off.

Thumb

Beg at center of palm, and pick up 12 sts in same manner as left thumb, pm for beg of rnd, sl 12 sts from scrap yarn to 2 more dpns, divide for 8 sts on each dpn. Join to work in rnds. Work foll chart 3 and complete as for left thumb. ✣

CHART 2

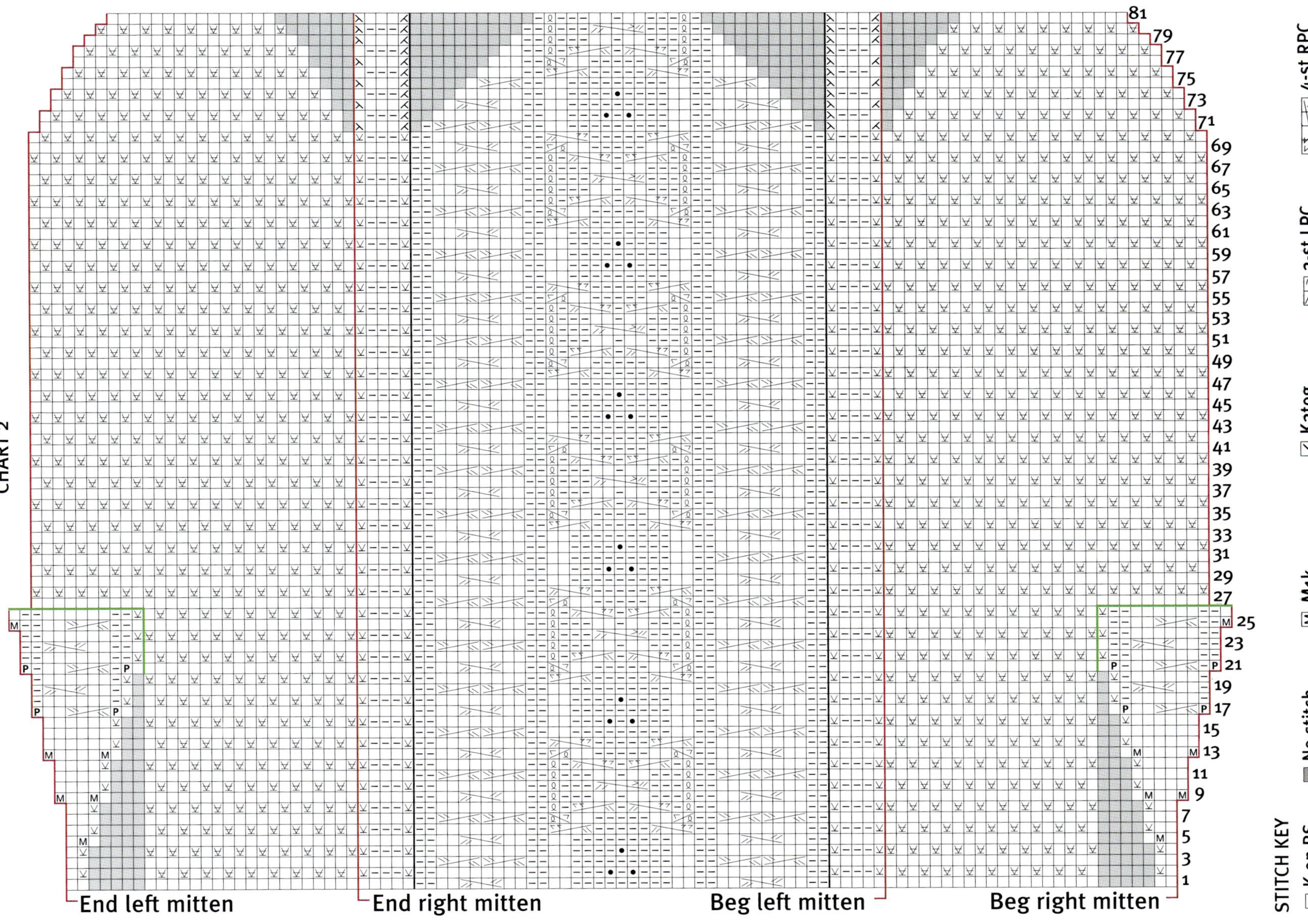

STITCH KEY

- K on RS
- P on RS
- K1 tbl
- No stitch
- Slip 1 wyif
- Slip 1 wyib
- M1k
- M1p
- MB
- K2tog
- Ssk
- 2-st RPC
- 2-st LPC
- 4-st RC
- 4-st LC
- 4-st RPC
- 4-st LPC
- 5-st LPC

Geometric Intarsia Mittens and Scarf

Michele Rose Orne's fun mittens make a bold statement when paired with a playful matching scarf. They're proof that you can never have too much color.

KNITTED MEASUREMENTS

Scarf

13½" x 50"/34.5cm x 127cm

Mittens

Hand circumference 9½"/24cm

Length 13½"/34cm

SIZE

Sized for adult woman.

MATERIALS

Original Yarn

2 1¾oz/50g skeins (each approx 65yd/60m) each of Classic Elite Yarns *Bazic* (wool) in #2972 light aqua (A) and #2955 rust (B) (4)

1 skein each in #2935 medium turquoise (C), #2992 teal (D), #2916 cream (E), #2945 taupe (F), #2061 coral (G), #2919 fuchsia (H), #2932 burgundy (I), #2902 celery (J) and #2908 olive (K)

Substitute Yarn

2 1¾oz/50g hanks (each approx 77yd/70m) each of Classic Elite Yarns *MinnowMerino* (superwash merino) in #4704 icy blue (A) and #4758 rouge (B) (4)

1 hank each in #4731 turquoise (C), #4720 aqua (D), #4716 lamb's white (E), #4778 bruin (F), #4788 tangerine (G), #4789 pinque (H), #4755 cerise (I), #4735 chartreuse (J) and #4781 green grass (K)

Scarf: One pair size 8 (5mm) needles OR SIZE TO OBTAIN GAUGE

Mittens: Set of 5 size 8 (5mm) double-pointed needles (dpns) OR SIZE TO OBTAIN GAUGE

Bobbins

Mittens: Stitch marker and 2 small stitch holders

GAUGE

15 sts and 22 rows = 4"/10cm over St st using size 8 (5mm) needles. TAKE TIME TO CHECK GAUGE.

NOTES

1. When working Scarf Chart, use a separate bobbin for each block of color. Bring new color under old color at each color change to prevent holes. Do not carry yarns not in use across back of work.

2. When working 2-color rnds of Mitten Chart, carry unused yarn across back of work. To prevent long, loose strands, twist the 2 yarns when the unused yarn must be carried over more than 3 sts.

SCARF

With A, cast on 51 sts.

Row 1 (RS) K2, *p2, k3; rep from * to last 4 sts, end p2, k2.

Row 2 P2, *k2, p3; rep from * to last 4 sts, end k2, p2.

Rep rows 1 and 2 once more, then rep row 1 once more.

Next row (WS) Purl.

Beg chart pat

Work rows 1–260 of Scarf Chart.

Next row (RS) With A, knit.

Beg with row 2, work in k3, p2 rib pat for 5 rows.

Bind off in rib.

RIGHT MITTEN

With A, cast on 35 sts, divided over 4 dpns. Place marker and join.

Beg k3, p2 rib pat

Rnd 1 *K3, p2; rep from * around.

Rnds 2–9 Rep rnd 1, inc 1 st on last rnd—36 sts.

Beg chart pat

Work rnds 1–41 of Mitten Chart.

Thumbhole placement

Rnd 42 With H, k2, sl next 6 sts to st holder, cast on 6 sts onto RH needle, k to end of rnd. Work through chart rnd 61.

Top of hand shaping

Divide sts between 2 dpns—18 sts on each dpn. Rnd 62 (dec rnd) [SKP, k to last 2 sts of dpn, k2tog] twice—16 sts on each dpn.

Next rnd Work even. Rep last 2 rnds 4 times more, then work dec rnd once more— 6 sts on each needle. Graft sts tog.

Thumb shaping

With dpn and G, k6 from st holder, pick up and k 1 st at side of opening, with another dpn, pick up and k6 sts along cast-on edge, and 1 st at side of opening—14 sts. K 9 rnds. Dec 1 st each side of each dpn every other rnd twice—3 sts on each dpn. Work 1 rnd even. Graft sts tog.

LEFT MITTEN

Work as for right mitten, reversing placement of thumbhole as foll:

Rnd 42 K28, sl 6 sts onto st holder, k2. ✣

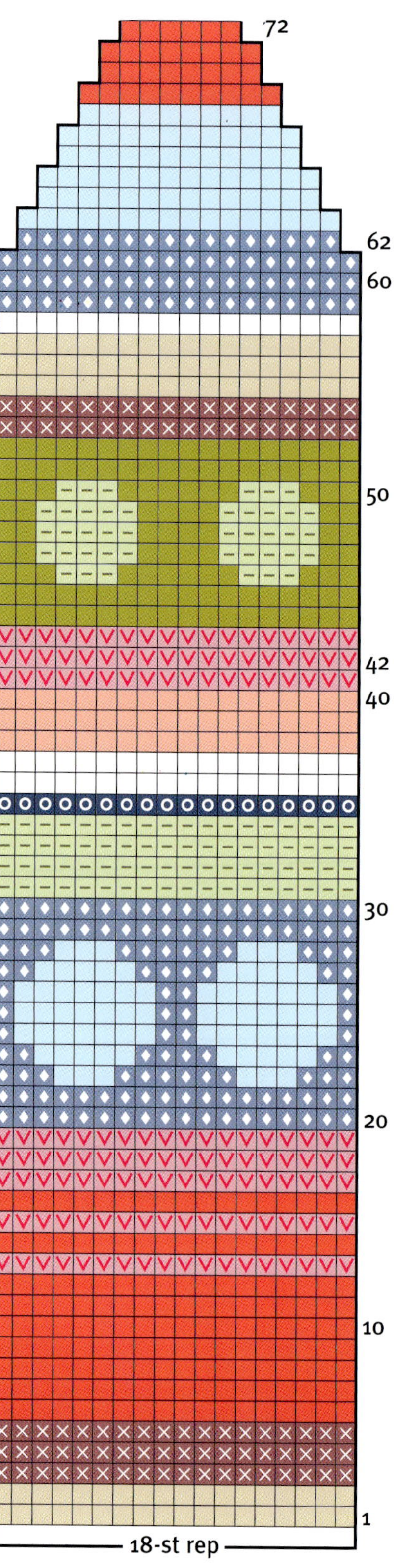

SCARF CHART, PART 1

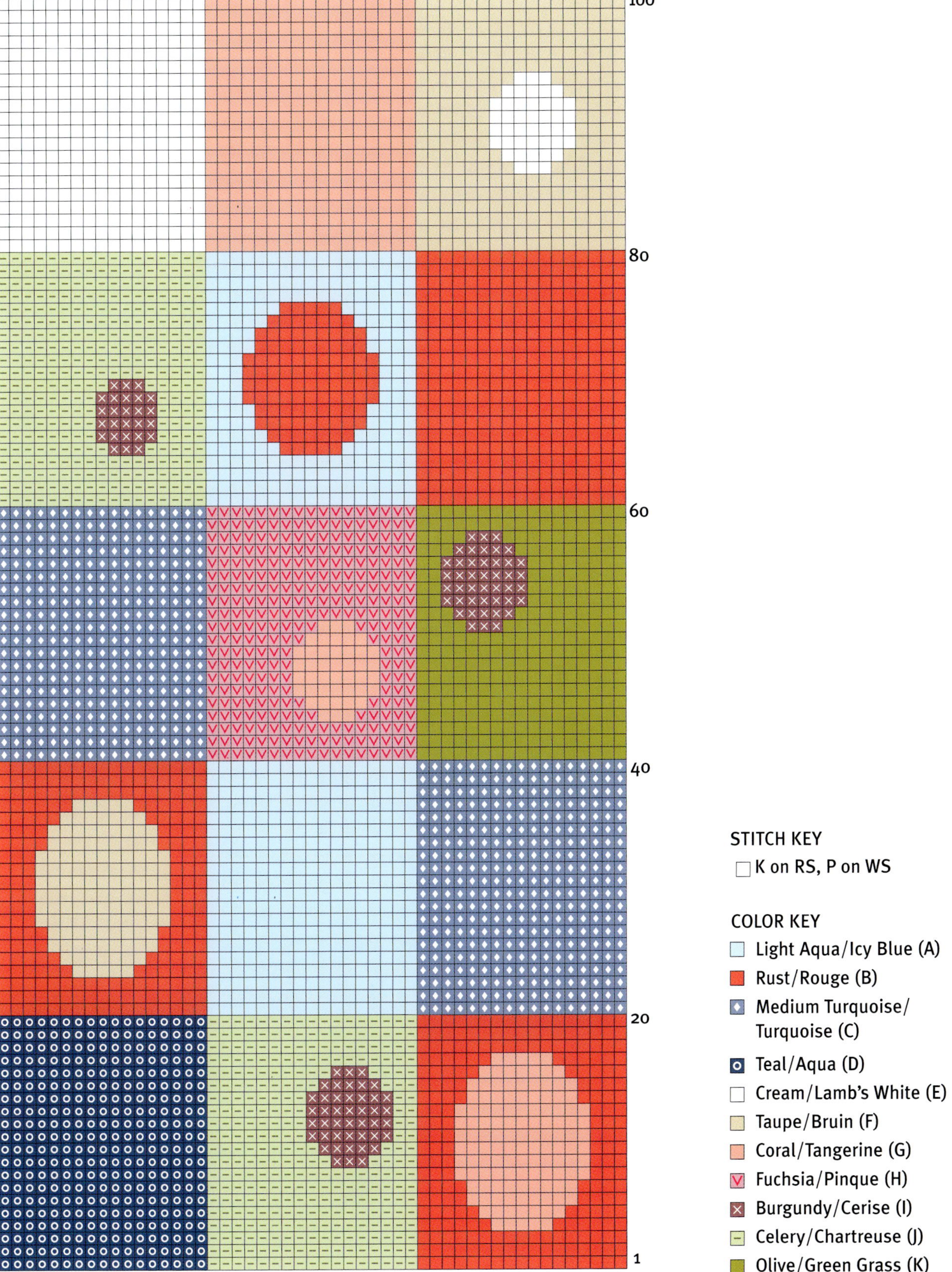
100
80
60
40
20
1
51 sts
STITCH KEY
K on RS, P on WS
COLOR KEY
Light Aqua/Icy Blue (A)
Rust/Rouge (B)
Medium Turquoise/Turquoise (C)
Teal/Aqua (D)
Cream/Lamb's White (E)
Taupe/Bruin (F)
Coral/Tangerine (G)
Fuchsia/Pinque (H)
Burgundy/Cerise (I)
Celery/Chartreuse (J)
Olive/Green Grass (K)

SCARF CHART, PART 2

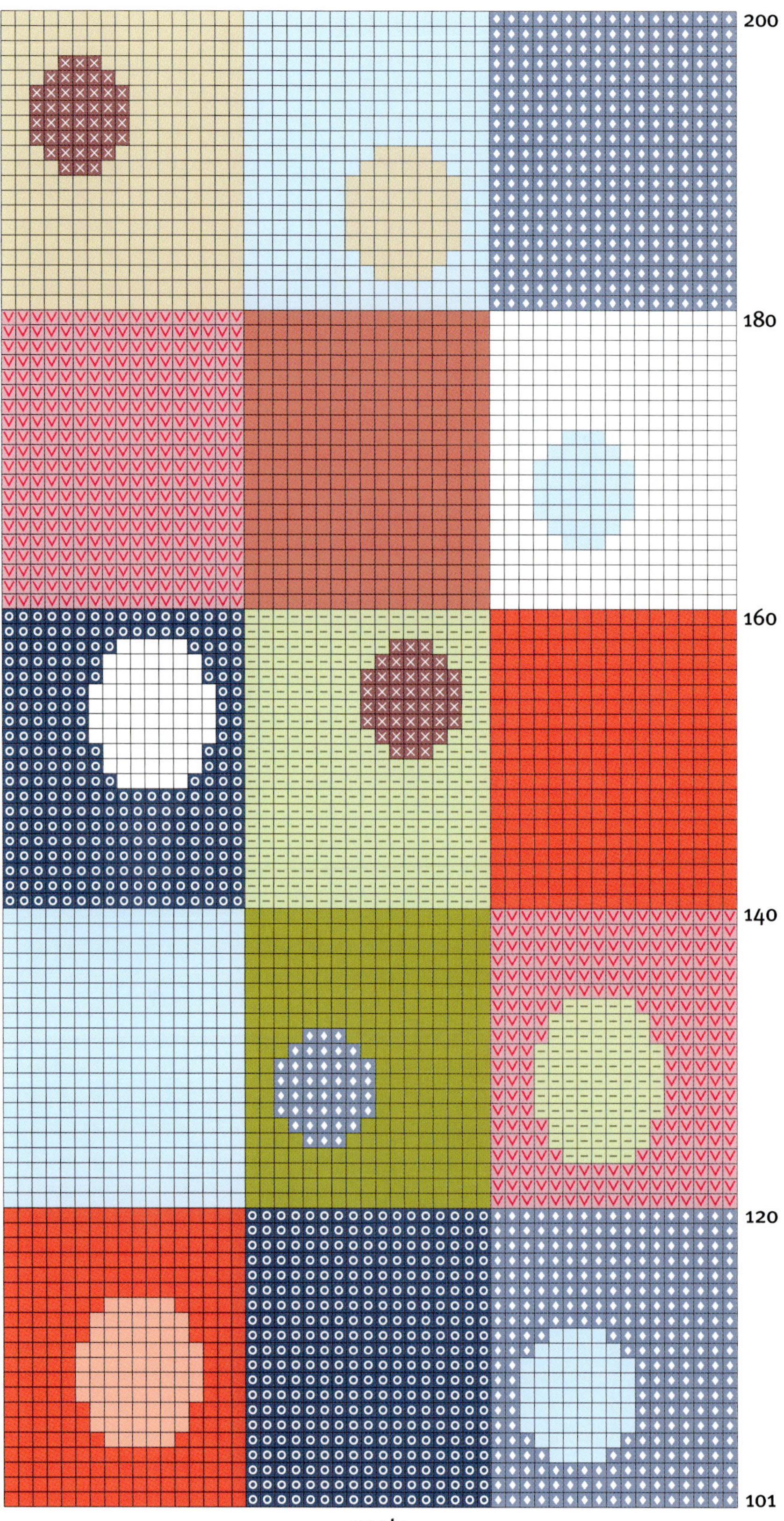

SCARF CHART, PART 3

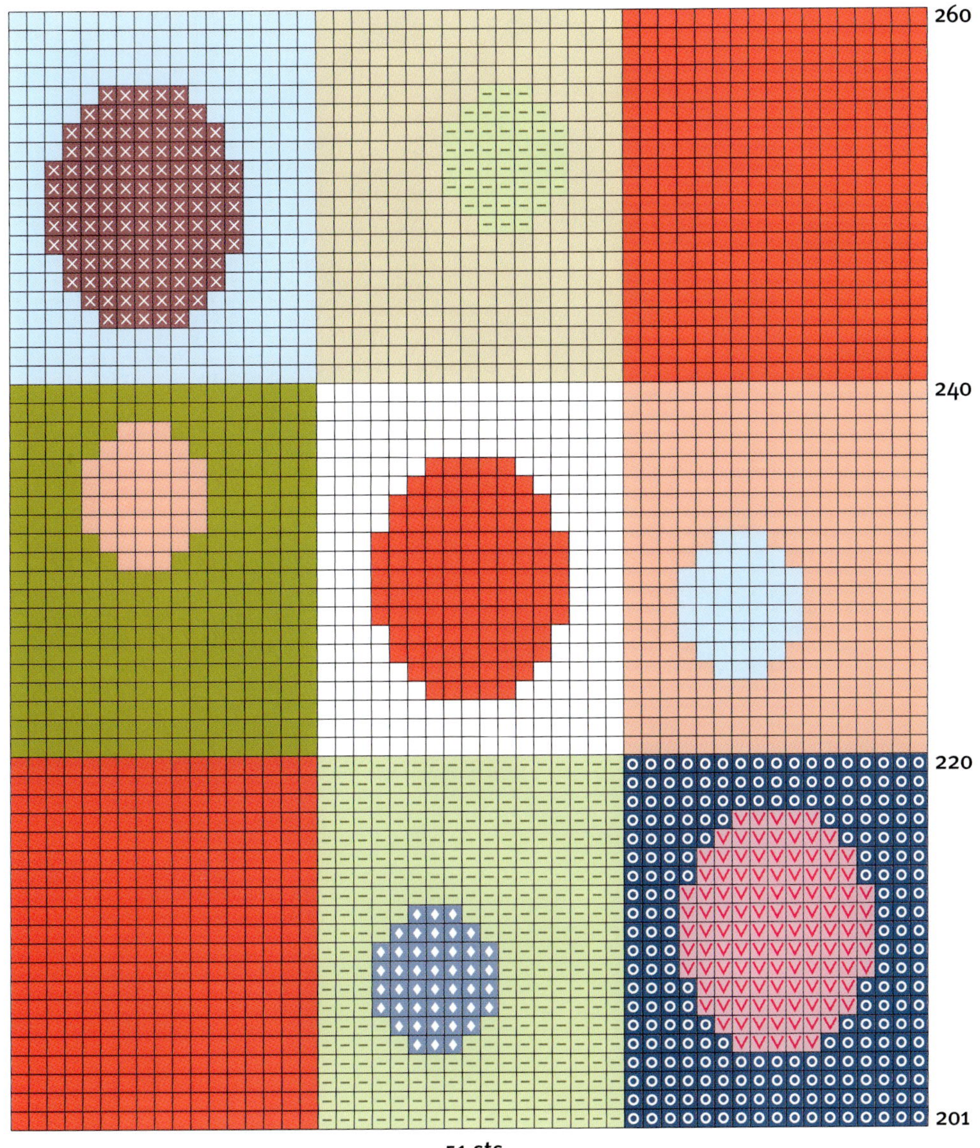

STITCH KEY

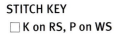

- K on RS, P on WS

COLOR KEY

- Light Aqua/Icy Blue (A)
- Rust/Rouge (B)
- Medium Turquoise/Turquoise (C)
- Teal/Aqua (D)
- Cream/Lamb's White (E)
- Taupe/Bruin (F)
- Coral/Tangerine (G)
- Fuchsia/Pinque (H)
- Burgundy/Cerise (I)
- Celery/Chartreuse (J)
- Olive/Green Grass (K)

Snowball Mittens

Knit in ultra-deep blue and a pale shade of silver, Elinor Brown's Fair Isle mittens make a graphic statement.

KNITTED MEASUREMENTS

Hand circumference (above thumb) 8"/20.5cm

Length 10½"/26.5cm

SIZE Sized for adult woman.

MATERIALS

1 2oz/55g hank (approx 400yd/366m) each of Jade Sapphire Exotic Fibres *Mongolian Cashmere 2-ply* (cashmere) in #44 deep denim (A) and #35 sterling (B) (2)

Set of 5 size 3 (3.25mm) double-pointed needles (dpns) OR SIZE TO OBTAIN GAUGE

Stitch marker and scrap yarn

GAUGES

38 sts and 36 rnds = 4"/10cm over chart pat using size 3 (3.25mm) needles. TAKE TIME TO CHECK GAUGE.

CORRUGATED RIB (over an even number of sts)

Rnd 1 *Bring B to front of work and p1, bring B to back of work, with A, k1; rep from * around.

Rep rnd 1 for corrugated rib.

LEFT MITTEN

With A, cast on 72 sts loosely. Place marker (pm) and join, being careful not to twist. Join B and work in corrugated rib until piece measures 1½"/4cm from beg.

Next rnd *[K1 B, k1 A] 3 times, with A, M1, k6, M1, [k1 B, k9 A] twice, [k1 B, k1 A] twice; rep from * once more—76 sts.

Beg chart 1

Work rnds 2–10 of chart 1 (working 38-st rep twice around), then rep rnds 1–10 twice more, work chart rnds 1–7 once more.

Thumb placement (see photo #1 on page 34)

Next rnd Work 24 sts in pat, join scrap yarn and k12, sl scrap yarn sts back to LH needle, work chart rnd 8 over all sts, including scrap yarn sts. Cont in pat until 10 rnds of chart have been worked 7 times from beg.

Top shaping

Next (dec) rnd Cont in pat as established, [k3, pm, ssk, k29, k2tog, pm, k2] twice—72 sts.

Next (dec) rnd [K3, sl marker, ssk, k to 2 sts before next marker, k2tog, sl marker, k2] twice—68 sts.

Rep last rnd 9 times more—32 sts. Cut yarn, leaving a 12"/30.5cm tail. Graft sts at mitten top tog.

Thumb

Read through instructions before beg to knit thumb.

Slip sts to dpn #1 and #2 and remove scrap yarn (see photos 2–4 on page 34)—24 sts. Join A and B.

Begin chart 2

Next rnd With RS of dpn #1 facing work chart rnd 1 as foll: K into front and back of first st with A, k1 A, k7 B, k3 A, then pick up and k 5 sts along side edge of opening as foll: [1 B, 1 A] twice, 1 B—18 sts on dpn #1; with RS of dpn #2 facing, cont with chart rnd 1 and k3 A, k7 B, k1 A, k into front and back of next st with A, then pick up and k 5 sts along side edge of opening as foll: 1 B, 1 A (pm for beg of chart rnd 2), 1 B, 1 A, 1 B—36 sts. Arrange sts comfortably on dpns, keeping marker in place. Cont to work 18-st rep of rnd 2 twice over 36 sts. Cont to follow chart 2 until rnd 26 has been completed—12 sts. Cut yarn leaving 6"/15cm tail. Graft sts at thumb top.

RIGHT MITTEN

Work as for left mitten, working thumb placement as foll:

Thumb placement

Next rnd Work 3 sts in pat, join scrap yarn, k12 with scrap yarn, sl scrap yarn sts back to LH needle, work rnd 8 across all sts, including scrap yarn sts. Complete as for left mitten.

Thumb

Slip sts to dpn #1 and #2 as for left thumb and remove scrap yarn—24 sts. Join A and B.

Beg chart 2

Next rnd With RS of dpn #1 facing work chart rnd 1 as foll: K3 A, k7 B, k1 A, k into front and back of next st with A, then pick up and k 5 sts along side edge of opening as foll: [1 B, 1 A] twice, 1 B—18 sts on dpn #1; with RS of dpn #2 facing, cont with chart rnd 1 and k into front and back of first st with A, k1 A, k7 B, k3 A, then pick up and k 5 sts along side edge of opening as foll: 1 B, 1 A, pm for beg chart rnd 2, 1 B, 1 A, 1 B—36 sts. Arrange sts comfortably on dpns, keeping marker in place. Cont to work 18-st rep of rnd 2 twice over 36 sts. Complete as for left thumb. ✣

PLACING THE THUMB INTO THE COLOR PATTERN

1. To place thumb, join scrap yarn and knit the next 12 sts. Slip scrap yarn sts back to LH needle and cont to foll chart. (Use a smooth scrap yarn in a contrasting color; it will be easier to remove later.)

2. When the hand of the mitten is complete, begin thumb by sliding dpn #1 into sts below scrap yarn, taking care to slip needles through the first leg of each st, skipping the second leg.

3. Next, slide dpn #2 into the 12 sts above the scrap yarn. Both needles and sts should be parallel, as shown.

4. Carefully remove scrap yarn, one st at a time, by inserting a tapestry needle through the first st and gently pulling the yarn through.

CHART 1

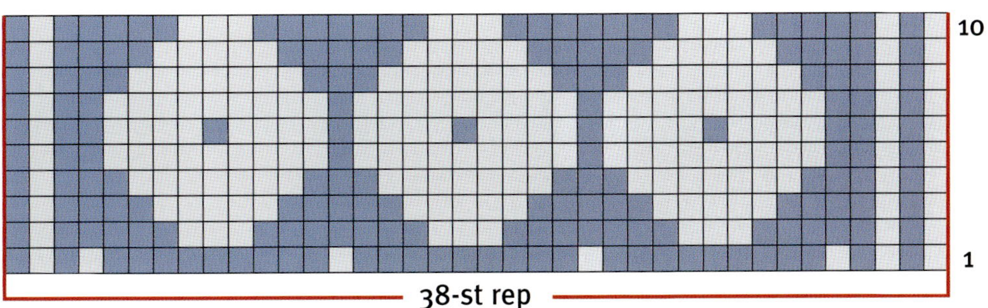

CHART 2

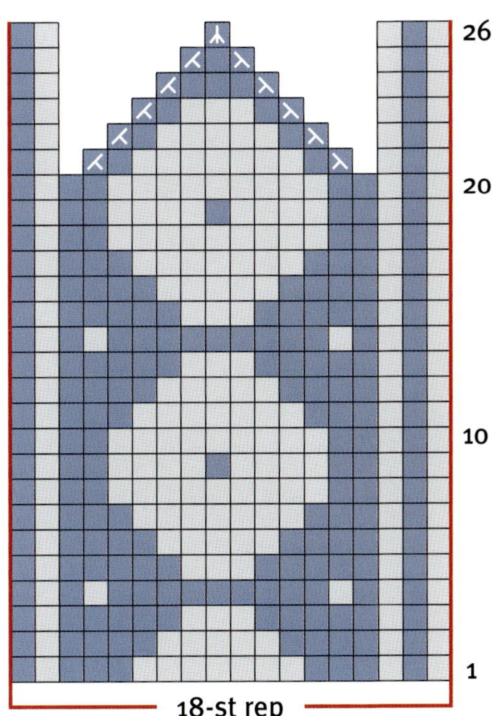

COLOR KEY

- Deep Denim (A)
- Sterling (B)

STITCH KEY

- K2tog
- Ssk
- S2KP

Tapestry Mittens

Inspired by colorful Central Asian textiles called *suzani,* Kristin Nicholas designed these long mittens to make a statement. With intricate edgings, embroidery, pom-poms and drawstrings, they definitely do.

■■■■□

KNITTED MEASUREMENTS

Hand circumference 7 (8)"/17.5 (20.5)cm

Length of cuff 9"/23cm

SIZE

Sized for Women's Small/Medium (Medium/Large) and shown in size Small/Medium.

MATERIALS

2 (3) 1¾oz/50g skeins (each approx 93yd/85m) of Nashua Handknits/Westminster Fibers, Inc. *Julia* (wool/kid mohair/alpaca) in #6085 geranium (MC) (4)

1 skein each in #3961 lady's mantle (A), #118 espresso (B) and #4936 blue thyme (C)

One pair size 7 (4.5mm) needles OR SIZE TO OBTAIN GAUGE

Set of 4 size 7 (4.5mm) double-pointed needles (dpns)

Stitch markers

GAUGE

20 sts and 27 rows = 4"/10cm over St st using size 7 (4.5mm) needles.

TAKE TIME TO CHECK GAUGE.

MITTENS (make 2)

With straight needles and MC, cast on 78 (91) sts.

Cuff

Row 1 (WS) Knit.

Row 2 *K5, S2KP, k5; rep from * to end—66 (77) sts.

Row 3 *K4, S2KP, k4; rep from * to end—54 (63) sts.

Row 4 *K3, S2KP, k3; rep from * to end—42 (49) sts. Change to dpns, dividing sts evenly between 3 needles. Place marker (pm), and join.

Rnd 1 With MC, purl.

Rnd 2 With A, knit.

Rnd 3 With A, purl.

Rnd 4 With MC, knit.

Rnd 5 With MC, purl dec 0 (1) st—42 (48) sts. Mark last rnd. Cont in St st until piece measures 1½"/4cm above marked rnd.

Next (dec) rnd [K1, k2tog, k15 (18), k2tog, k1] twice—38 (44) sts. Work even until piece measures 2¾"/7cm above marked rnd.

Next (dec) rnd [K1, k2tog, k13 (16), k2tog, k1] twice—34 (40) sts. Work even until piece measures 3½"/9cm above marked rnd.

Change to A.

Eyelet band

Rnd 1 Knit.

Rnds 2 and 3 Purl

Rnd 4 Knit, inc 1 (0) st—35 (40) sts.

For size Small/Medium only

Rnd 5 [K2, k2tog, yo, k3, k2tog, yo] 3 times, [k2, k2tog, yo] twice.

For size Medium/Large only

Rnd 5 [K1, k2tog, yo, k1] 10 times.

For both sizes

Rnd 6 Knit.

Rnds 7 and 8 Purl. Change to MC.

Hand

Work even until piece measures 7½"/19cm

DIAGRAM 1

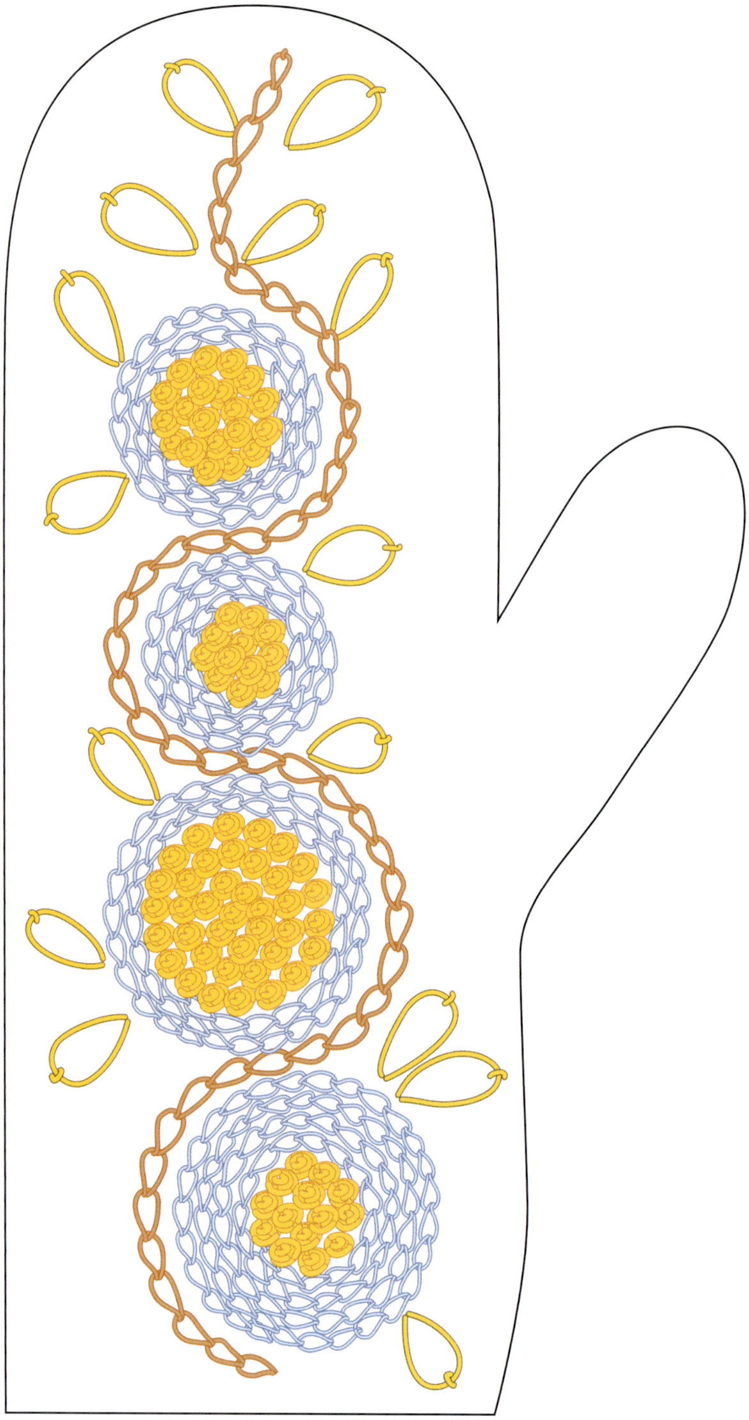

COLOR KEY

- Lady's Mantle (A)
- Espresso (B)
- Blue Thyme (C)

STITCH KEY

- Chain stitch
- Lazy daisy stitch
- French knot

above marked rnd.

Thumb gusset

Inc rnd 1 K18 (20), pm, M1, pm, k17 (20)—36 (41) sts.

Next rnd Knit.

Inc rnd 2 K to first marker, sl marker, M1, k to next marker, M1, sl marker, k to end—38 (43) sts. Rep inc rnd 2 every other rnd 5 (6) times more—48 (55) sts.

Next rnd Knit.

Next rnd K to first marker, place 13 (15) gusset sts on scrap yarn (removing markers), k to end—35 (40) sts. Work even until piece measures 13½"/34cm above marked rnd.

Top shaping

Rnd 1 *K2, k2tog; rep from * around, end k 3 (0)—27 (30) sts.

Rnds 2, 4 and 6 Knit.

Rnd 3 (dec rnd) *K1, k2tog; rep from * around—18 (20) sts.

Rnd 5 (dec rnd) [K2tog] 9 (10) times—9 (10) sts.

Rnd 7 (dec rnd) [K2tog] 4 (5) times, end k 1 (0)—5 sts. Cut yarn, leaving a 6"/15cm tail. Thread through rem sts and cinch tightly to close.

Thumb

Place 13 (15) thumb gusset sts on 2 dpns.

Next rnd Join yarn and knit across sts, then pick up and k 1 st at base of hand—14 (16) sts. Divide sts evenly over 3 dpns. Pm and join. Work in St st for 1⅝"/4cm.

Top shaping

Next (dec) rnd [K2tog] 7 (8) times—7 (8) sts.

Next rnd Knit.

Next (dec) rnd [K2tog] 3 (4) times, end k 1 (0)—4 sts. Cut yarn, leaving a 6"/15cm tail. Finish as for top of mitten.

FINISHING

Sew lower cuff seam.

Embroidery

Use 2 strands of yarn throughout. Embroider back hand of left mitten foll diagram 1 as foll: With A, embroider French knots for centers of flowers. Using C, embroider concentric circles of chain sts around French knot centers for petals. With B, embroider chain st vine, beg just below first flower and ending at top of mitten. With 1 strand each of A and B tog, embroider lazy daisy leaves. With 1 strand each A and B, foll diagram 2 and embroider chain st scroll pat on cuff of left mitten. For right mitten, photocopy diagrams 1 and 2, and reverse the images.

Ties (make 2)

With straight needles and B, cast on 50 sts. Bind off all sts knitwise. Weave each tie through eyelets around wrist, beg and ending on side opposite thumb. Make four 2½"/6.5cm diameter pom-poms. Sew pom-poms to ends of ties. ✣

DIAGRAM 2

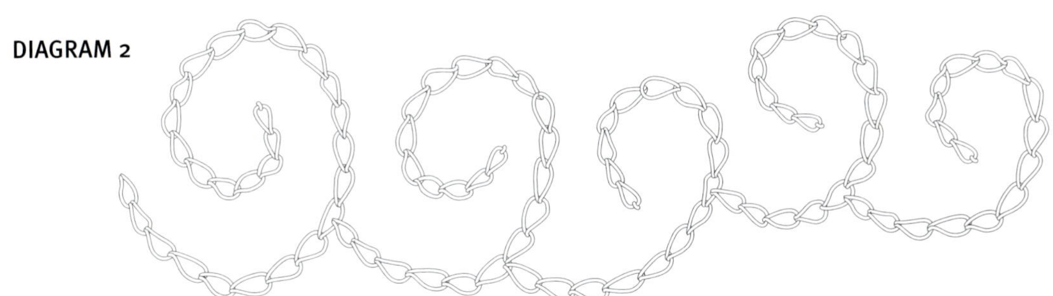

Hugs and Kisses Mittens

With their complementary colors and playful pattern of Xs and Os, Tanis Gray's Fair Isle mittens will warm the coldest day.

KNITTED MEASUREMENTS

Hand circumference 7½"/19cm

Length of cuff 2¾"/7cm

SIZE

Sized for adult woman.

MATERIALS

1 1¾oz/50g ball (approx 175yd/160m) each of Claudia Hand Painted Yarns *Fingering* (merino wool) in citrus (A), baby boy (B), undyed (C) and cherries (D) (1)

Set of 4 size 1 (2.25mm) double-pointed needles (dpns) OR SIZE TO OBTAIN GAUGE

Size C/2 (2.75mm) crochet hook

Stitch markers and scrap yarn

GAUGE

34 sts and 41 rnds = 4"/10cm over chart pat using size 1 (2.25mm) needles.

TAKE TIME TO CHECK GAUGE.

PROVISIONAL CAST-ON

Using scrap yarn and crochet hook, ch the number of cast-on sts, plus a few extra. Cut yarn and pull the tail through the last chain to secure. With knitting needle and yarn, pick up the required number of cast-on sts through the "purl bumps" on the back of the chain. Be careful not to split the waste yarn, as this makes it difficult to pull out the chain at the end. When it's time to remove the chain, pull out the tail from the last chain st. Gently and slowly pull on the tail to unravel the crochet stitches, carefully placing each released knit st on a needle as you go.

LEFT MITTEN

With A, cast on 60 sts, using provisional cast-on. Divide sts evenly over 3 needles. Place marker (pm), and join.

Picot edging

Rnds 1–3 Knit.

Rnd 4 (eyelet rnd) *Yo, k2tog; rep from * around.

Rnds 5–7 Knit.

Join hem

Place cast-on sts onto needles (removing chain). Fold hem to WS at eyelet rnd so that needles are tog. Join as foll: *Insert RH needle into 1 st on front needle and 1 cast-on st and k these 2 sts tog; rep from * around.

Change to B and k 2 rnds.

Beg chart 1

Work rnds 1–17 of chart 1. With B, k 2 rnds.

With D, k 1 rnd.

Hand

Next (inc) rnd With B, k1, M1, k28, M1, k2, M1, k28, M1, k1—64 sts.

Beg chart 2

Rnd 1 [With B, k1, work 10-st rep of chart 3 times, with B, k1] twice.

Cont in pats as established through chart rnd 8.

Thumb opening

Chart rnd 9 Work 30 sts, place last 11 sts worked on scrap yarn (for thumb), work to end.

Chart rnd 10 Work 19 sts, cast on 11 sts over

thumb sts, work to end. Cont in pats as established through rnd 7 of 4th chart rep.

Top shaping

Next rnd Work 32 sts, pm, work to end.

Next (dec) rnd [Ssk, work to 2 sts before marker, k2tog] twice—60 sts.

Rep dec rnd every rnd 12 times more—12 sts. Cut yarn. Using B, graft or use 3-needle bind-off to join sts (see page 144).

Thumb

Place first 10 sts on scrap yarn onto first needle, then place last st on 2nd needle. With 2nd needle and B, pick up and k 4 sts along side edge of thumb opening, with 3rd needle, pick up and k 11 sts along cast-on edge of opening, then pick up and k 4 sts along opposite side edge of opening—30 sts. Divide sts evenly between 2nd and 3rd needles (10 sts on each needle). Join and pm for beg of rnds between first and 3rd needles.

Beg chart 2

Beg with 4th st of chart, work in chart pat around. Work through chart rnd 16, then rep rnds 1–10 once more.

Top shaping

Next (dec) rnd With B, [k2tog] 15 times—15 sts. Cut yarn, leaving a 6"/15cm tail. Thread through rem sts and cinch tightly to close.

RIGHT MITTEN

Work as for left mitten to thumb opening.

Thumb opening

Chart rnd 9 Work 13 sts, place last 11 sts worked on scrap yarn (for thumb), work to end.

Chart rnd 10 Work 2 sts, cast on 11 sts over thumb sts, work to end. Cont as for left mitten.

Thumb

Work as for left mitten, working chart 2 as foll:

Beg chart 2

Beg with 7th st of chart, work in chart pat around. Complete as for left mitten. ✣

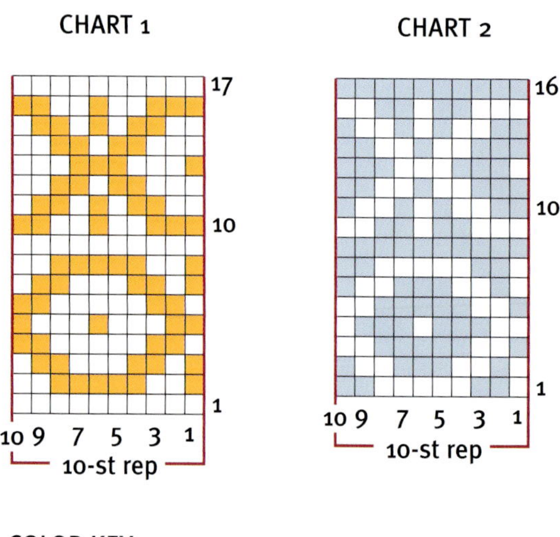

COLOR KEY

- Citrus (A)
- Baby Boy (B)
- Undyed (C)

Alpine Mittens

Jewel-toned handpainted yarns and a gorgeous Fair Isle design add up to evergreen style. The corrugated-rib cuff sets off the tree motif nicely.

KNITTED MEASUREMENTS

Hand circumference (above thumb) 8"/20.5cm

Length 9¼"/23.5cm

SIZE

Sized for adult woman.

MATERIALS

1 3½oz/100g skein (approx 188yd/172m) each of Artyarns *Ultramerino 8* (wool) in #225 blue (A) and #234 green (B) (4)

Set of 5 each sizes 4 and 5 (3.5 and 3.75mm) double-pointed needles (dpns) OR SIZE TO OBTAIN GAUGE

Scrap yarn

Stitch marker and tapestry needle

GAUGE

23 sts and 25 rnds = 4"/10cm over chart pat (after blocking) using larger needles.

TAKE TIME TO CHECK GAUGE.

STITCH GLOSSARY

(**Note** When working incs, insert LH needle under the color strand that corresponds to the new st.)

M1R Insert LH needle from back to front under strand between last st worked and next st on LH needle. K into front loop to twist st.

M1L Insert LH needle from front to back under strand between last st worked and next st on LH needle. K into back loop to twist st.

K2, P1 CORRUGATED RIB (over a multiple of 3 sts)

Rnd 1 *K2 A, bring B to front of work and p1,

bring B to back of work; rep from * around.

Rep rnd 1 for k2, p1 corrugated rib.

LEFT MITTEN

Cuff

With smaller needles and A, cast on 42 sts, divided over 4 needles. Place marker (pm) and join, being careful not to twist.

Work in corrugated rib until cuff measures 2"/5cm from beg.

Next rnd *K2 B, k1 A; rep from * around.

Next rnd With A, k 1 rnd. Change to larger needles.

Next (inc) rnd With A, [k9, k into front and back of next st (kfb), k10, kfb] twice—46 sts.

Hand

Beg charts 1, 2 and gusset chart

Rnd 1 Work 23 sts of chart 1 (back of hand), work 23 sts of chart 2 (palm).

Rnd 2 M1R (for center of gusset), work rnd 2 of charts 1 and 2 as established.

Beg gusset chart

Rnd 3 Work 1 st of gusset chart (the center st on chart), work in pat to end. Cont in pats through chart rnd 21—19 gusset sts.

Rnd 22 Place 19 gusset sts on scrap yarn, cont to foll charts 1 and 2. When rnd 45 of charts 1 and 2 is complete, cut yarn, leaving a 12"/30.5cm tail of A.

Thumb

Move 19 thumb sts from scrap yarn to dpns, rejoin yarn, leaving long tail of A for sewing up.

Beg thumb chart

Rnd 1 With A, M1R, k1, [k1 B, k2 A] twice, k1 B, k3 A, [k1 B, k2 A] twice, k1 B, k1 A—20 sts.

Cont in pat as established through chart rnd 8—16 sts.

Next rnd With A, *k2tog; rep from * to end—8 sts.

Cut yarn and draw through rem sts.

RIGHT MITTEN

Cuff

Work as for left mitten.

Hand

Beg charts 2, 1 and gusset

(**Note** To mirror the tree image, work chart 1 from left to right.)

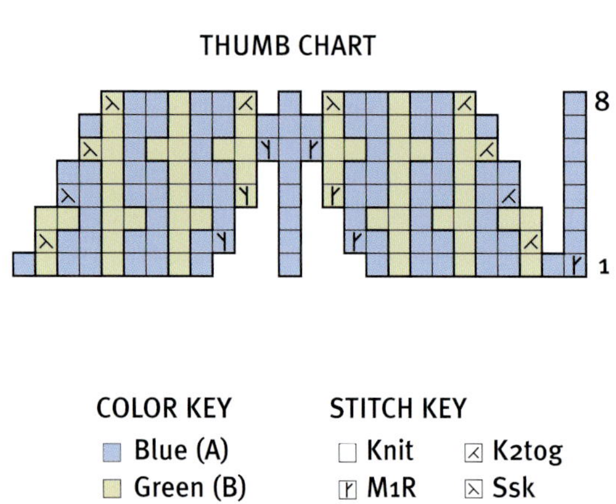

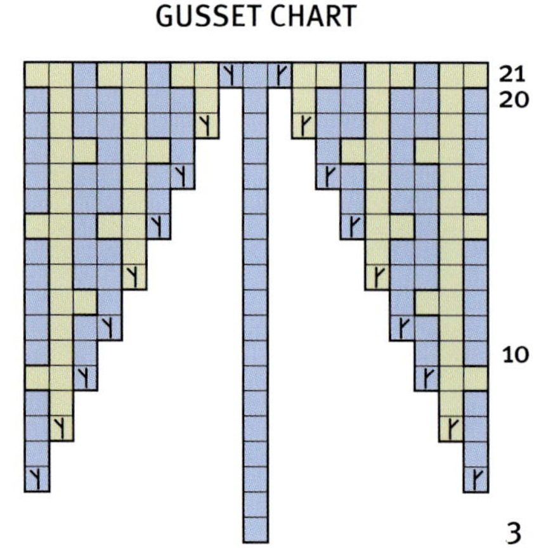

CHART 1 (Back of Hand)

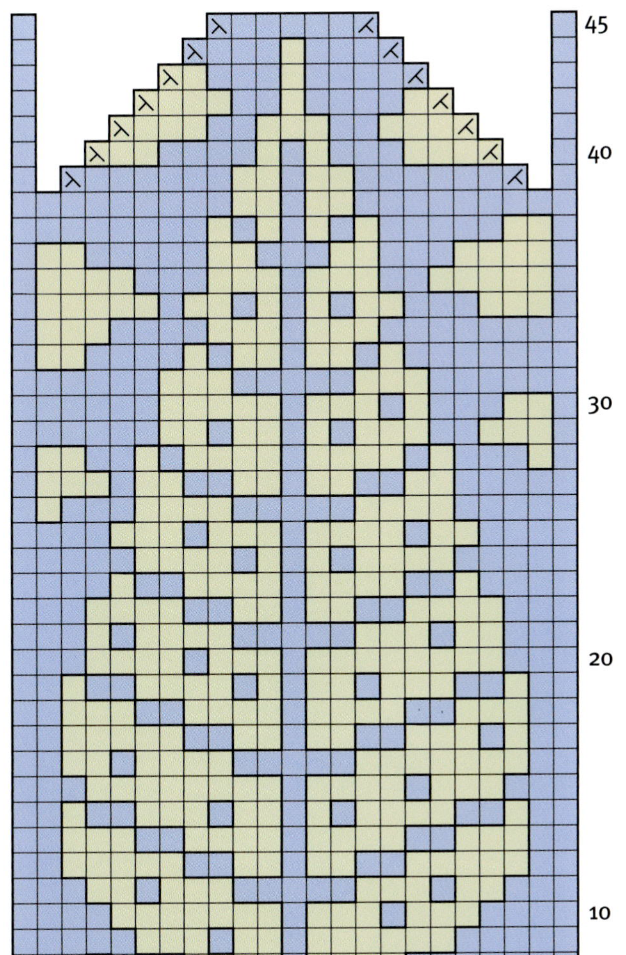

CHART 2 (Palm)

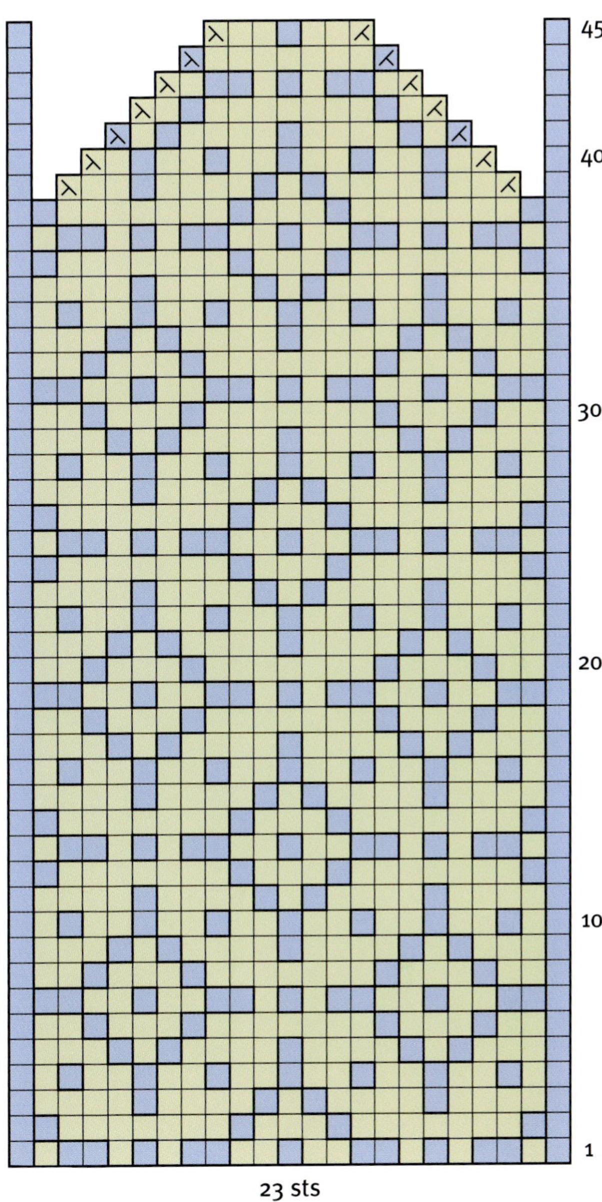

ONE BUSHEL

Rnd 1 Work chart 2 (palm) over 23 sts, work chart 1 (back of hand) over 23 sts. Cont same as for left mitten, work M1R and gusset chart at beg of rnd before chart 2.

FINISHING

With tails of A and tapestry needle, graft mitten tops. Close gaps between thumb and hand. ✣

K2, P1 CORRUGATED RIB WORKED IN THE ROUND

1. With both strands at the back of the work, bring the strand for the knit stitch over the second color, as shown, and knit two stitches.

2. Bring the strand for the purl stitch under the first color, as shown, and then in the front of the work, and purl the next stitch.

3. When the purl stitch has been worked, be sure to bring the yarn to the back, between the needles, before picking up the strand for the next knit stitch.

4. When the color changes are worked correctly, the wrong side of the work will have an even, woven appearance, as shown.

Felted Pom-Pom Set

Linda Cyr's bright blue felted mittens are three times as fun when worn with a matching hat and coordinating scarf.

KNITTED MEASUREMENTS

Hat

Circumference 20"/51cm (after felting)

Length from tip of hat to folded-up brim 14"/35.5cm (after felting)

Scarf

Length 66"/167.5cm

Width 6"/15cm

Mittens

Hand circumference 9"/23cm (after felting)

Length 9"/23cm (after felting)

SIZE

Sized for adult woman.

MATERIALS

Original Yarn

4 1¾oz/50g balls (each approx 108yd/100m) of Dale of Norway *Heilo* (wool) in #5545 blue (A) (3)

4 1¾oz/50g balls (each approx 116yd/106m) of Dale of Norway *Falk* (superwash wool) in #5545 blue (B) (3)

1 1¾oz/50g ball (approx 126yd/115m) each of Dale of Norway *Tiur* (mohair/wool) in #2526 goldenrod (C), #4027 red (D), #4545 raspberry (E) (3)

Substitute Yarn

4 1¾oz/50g balls (each approx 108yd/100m) of Dale of Norway *Heilo* (wool) in #5646 blue (A) (3)

1 ball each of *Heilo* in #2427 gold (C), #4018 red (D) and #4227 cranberry (E) (3)

4 1¾oz/50g balls (each approx 116yd/106m) of Dale of Norway *Falk* (superwash wool) in #5646 blue (B) (3)

One pair size 6 (4mm) needles OR SIZE TO OBTAIN GAUGE

Size 6 (4mm) circular needle, 24"/60cm long

Set of 4 size 6 (4mm) double-pointed needles (dpns)

Size G/6 (4mm) crochet hook

Stitch markers and holder

GAUGES

20 sts and 26 rows = 4"/10cm over St st using size 6 (4mm) needles and *Heilo* (before felting).

26 sts = 4"/10cm over scarf pattern st using size 6 (4mm) needles and *Falk* (before felting).

TAKE TIME TO CHECK GAUGES.

NOTE

Scarf is not felted.

FELTING

Place hat, mittens and bobbles in washing machine set to hot wash/cold rinse with low water level. Add ¼ cup baking soda and 1 tablespoon dishwashing detergent at beg of wash cycle. Repeat cycle, if necessary, until knitted pieces are felted to desired size. Tumble dry on high. Block with steam to shape.

BOBBLES

For hat, make 8 with C, 6 with D, and 6 with E.

For mittens, make 6 each with C, D and E.

For scarf, make 14 each with C, D and E.

Cast on 1 st.

Row 1 (RS) [K1, yo, k1] into st—3 sts.

Rows 2, 4, 6, 7, 9 and 11 Knit.

Row 3 [K into front and back of st (kfb)] 3 times—6 sts.

Row 5 [K1, kfb] 3 times—9 sts.

Row 8 [K1, k2tog] 3 times—6 sts.

Row 10 [K2tog] 3 times—3 sts.

Row 12 SKP. Cut yarn, leaving a 12"/30.5cm tail, pull yarn end through st. Use yarn end to sew side seam.

HAT

Side piece

With circular needle and A, cast on 126 sts. Place marker (pm) and join, being careful not to twist.

Rnd 1 Knit.

Rnd 2 Purl.

Rnds 3–6 Rep rnds 1 and 2 twice more.

Rnd 7 [M1, k9] 14 times—140 sts. Work even in garter st until piece measures 5½"/14cm from beg. Bind off.

Crown

With straight needles and A, cast on 36 sts. Work back and forth in rows as foll:

Beg seed st

Row 1 (RS) Sl 1 knitwise, *k1, p1; rep from *, end k1.

Row 2 Sl 1 purlwise, *p1, k1; rep from *, end p1. Rep last 2 rows 34 times more. Bind off.

FINISHING

Hold crown and top edge of side piece with WS tog. With crochet hook and A, work 1 rnd sl st through both thicknesses to join. Felt hat as described at beg of instructions. Sew 1 bobble under each corner of crown, using 2 C bobbles and 1 bobble each in D and E. Sew a C bobble at top of crown.

Sew rem 15 bobbles around lower edge of hat, alternating colors.

MITTENS (make 2)

With dpn and B, cast on 45 sts, divided evenly over 3 dpns. Pm and join, being careful not to twist sts.

Beg rib pat

Rnd 1 [K2, p3] 9 times.

Rnd 2 [K2, p1, k1, p1] 9 times.

Rnds 3–16 Rep last 2 rnds 7 times more. Change to A and St st.

Rnd 17 K6, [M1, k4] 9 times, end k3—54 sts.

Rnd 18 and all even rnds (Unless otherwise indicated) Knit.

Rnd 19 K6, pm, M1, k2, M1, pm, k to end—56 sts.

Rnd 21 K6, sl marker, M1, k to marker, M1, sl marker, k to end—58 sts.

Rnds 22–39 Rep rnds 20 and 21 nine times more—76 sts.

Rnd 41 K7, place next 22 sts on holder, cast on 4 sts, k to end—58 sts.

Rnd 43 Knit.

Rnd 45 K5, k2tog, k2, ssk, k to end—56 sts.

Rnd 47 K4, k2tog, k2, ssk, k to end—54 sts.

Rnds 48–71 Knit.

Rnd 72 (dec rnd) [K7, k2tog] 6 times—48 sts.

Rnds 73 and 74 Knit.

Rnds 75–83 Rep rnds 72–74 three times more, working 1 fewer st between decs each dec rnd—30 sts.

Rnd 84 [K3, k2tog] 6 times—24 sts.

Rnd 85 Knit.

Rnd 86 [K2, k2tog] 6 times—18 sts.

Rnd 87 Knit.

Rnd 88 [K1, k2tog] 6 times—12 sts.

Rnd 89 [K2tog] 6 times—6 sts. Cut yarn, thread onto tapestry needle, draw through rem 6 sts and pull closed.

Thumb

Rnd 1 With dpn and B, pick up 4 sts along cast-on edge at thumb opening, k 22 sts from holder—26 sts, divided over 3 dpns.

Rnd 2 Knit.

Rnd 3 Ssk, k2, k2tog, k to end—24 sts.

Rnds 4–7 Rep rnds 2 and 3 twice more—20 sts.

Rnds 8–23 Knit.

Rnd 24 [K2, k2tog] 5 times—15 sts.

Rnd 25 [K1, k2tog] 5 times—10 sts.

Rnd 26 [K2tog] 5 times—5 sts. Cut yarn, thread

onto tapestry needle, draw through rem 5 sts, pull closed.

FINISHING

Felt hat as described at beg of instructions. Sew 9 bobbles along last row of ribbing on each mitten, placing 1 bobble in each purl section, and alternating colors.

SCARF

With straight needles and B, cast on 6 sts.

Row 1 K5, p1.

Row 2 (and even rows through row 38) K1, M1, k to end.

Row 3 K5, p2.

Row 5 K5, p3.

Row 7 K5, p4.

Row 9 K5, p5.

Row 11 Cast on 5 sts, k5, p5, k5, p1.

Row 13 K5, p5, k5, p2.

Row 15 K5, p5, k5, p3.

Row 17 K5, p5, k5, p4.

Row 19 [K5, p5] twice.

Row 21 Cast on 5 sts, k5, [p5, k5] twice, p1.

Row 23 K5, [p5, k5] twice, p2.

Row 25 K5, [p5, k5] twice, p3.

Row 27 K5, [p5, k5] twice, p4.

Row 29 [K5, p5] 3 times.

Rows 31–39 Work as for rows 21–29, except work 1 more 10-st rep.

Row 40 (and even rows through row 358) K1, M1, k to last 2 sts, k2tog.

Row 41 P4, [k5, p5] 3 times, k5, p1.

Row 43 P3, [k5, p5] 3 times, k5, p2.

Row 45 P2, [k5, p5] 3 times, k5, p3.

Row 47 P1, [k5, p5] 3 times, k5, p4.

Row 49 [K5, p5] 4 times.

Rows 50–359 Rep rows 40–49 31 times more.

Row 360 (and even rows through row 368) K to last 2 sts, k2tog.

Row 361 P4, [k5, p5] 3 times, k5.

Row 363 P3, [k5, p5] 3 times, k5.

Row 365 P2, [k5, p5] 3 times, k5.

Row 367 P1, [k5, p5] 3 times, k5.

Row 369 [K5, p5] 3 times, k5.

Row 370 Bind off 5 sts, k to last 2 sts, k2tog.

Row 371 P4, [k5, p5] twice, k5.

Row 372 (and even rows through row 378) K to last 2 sts, k2tog.

Row 373 P3, [k5, p5] twice, k5.

Row 375 P2, [k5, p5] twice, k5.

Row 377 P1, [k5, p5] twice, k5.

Row 379 [K5, p5] twice, k5.

Row 380 Bind off 5 sts, k to last 2 sts, k2tog.

Row 381 P4, k5, p5, k5.

Row 382 (and even rows to row 388) K to last 2 sts, k2tog.

Row 383 P3, k5, p5, k5.

Row 385 P2, k5, p5, k5.

Row 387 P1, k5, p5, k5.

Row 389 K5, p5, k5.

Row 390 Bind off 5 sts, k to last 2 sts, k2tog.

Row 391 P4, k5.

Rows 392, 394, 396 and 398 K to last 2 sts, k2tog.

Row 393 P3, k5.

Row 395 P2, k5.

Row 397 P1, k5.

Row 399 K5.

Bind off.

FINISHING

Sew 1 E bobble in each of 4 outer points at ends of scarf. Sew 1 E and 1 C bobble on each of rem 2 points on each end of scarf. Sew 17 bobbles evenly spaced along each side of scarf, beg and end with C bobble. ✣

Fulled Mittens and Hat

Kristin Slade's fulled gauntlet mittens and matching hat are elegant pieces on their own—and even more so when you add floral embroidery, pom-poms and tassels.

KNITTED MEASUREMENTS

Mittens

Length from wrist to tip 12½"/32cm (before fulling)

Length from wrist to tip 10¾"/27cm (after fulling)

Hat

Circumference 23¾"/60cm (before fulling)

Circumference 20¾"/52.5cm (after fulling)

SIZE

Sized for adult woman.

MATERIALS

Original Yarn

3 3½ oz/100g hanks (each approx 127yd/116m) of Classic Elite Yarns *Montera* (llama/wool) in #3897 olive (MC) (4)
2 hanks in #3813 black (CC)
1 1¾oz/50g ball (approx 95yd/87m) each of Classic Elite Yarns *Tapestry* (wool/mohair) in #2254 purple (A), #2278 taupe (B), #2216 white (C), #2235 moss green (D), #2215 dark green (E) and #2234 raspberry (F) (4)

Substitute Yarn

3 3½oz/100g hanks (each approx 127yd/116m) of Classic Elite Yarns *Montera* (llama/wool) in #3840 tuscan hills (MC) (4)
2 hanks in #3813 black (CC)
1 1¾oz/50g ball (approx 150yd/137m) each of Classic Elite Yarns *Princess* (merino/viscose/ cashmere/ angora/nylon) in #3495 privileged plum (A), #3438 noble nutmeg (B), #3416 natural (C), #3460 greatest green (D), #3415 superior spruce (E) and #3455 patrician port (F) (4)
Set of 4 size 10½ (6.5mm) double-pointed needles (dpns) OR SIZE TO OBTAIN GAUGE
Stitch markers and holders
Tapestry needle

GAUGE

(Before fulling) 14 sts and 17 rnds = 4"/10cm over St st and MC using size 10½ (6.5mm) needles.

(After fulling) 16 sts and 18 rnds = 4"/10cm over St st and MC using size 10½ (6.5mm) needles.
TAKE TIME TO CHECK GAUGES.

NOTE

To work a gauge swatch, with MC, cast on 35 sts, divided over 3 dpns. Yo 3 times and join.

Rnd 1 K35, drop yo's from needle, yo 3 times. Rep rnd 1 until piece measures 6"/15cm from beg. Bind off. Cut along yo's to make a flat swatch. With heavy cotton thread, baste a 5"/12.5cm square at center of swatch. Set washing machine to hot wash/cold rinse, and wash cycle to 6 minutes. Add swatch, small towel (for abrasion) and a small amount of liquid laundry detergent. Wash swatch and spin dry. Basted square should measure about 4½"/11.5cm.

MITTENS

With dpn and MC, cast on 50 sts, divided over 3 dpns. Mark sts 25 and 50 for edge sts. Join to work in rnds.

Rnds 1–4 Purl.

Rnds 5–9 Knit.

Rnd 10 [K2tog, k to 2 sts before marked st, ssk, k marked st] twice—46 sts.

Rnd 11 Knit.

Rnd 12 Rep rnd 10—42 sts.

Rnds 13–15 Knit.

Rnds 16–19 Purl.

Rnd 20 Knit. **Rnd 21** Rep rnd 10—38 sts.

Rnds 22 and 23 Knit.

Thumb opening

Rnd 24 K14, k7 and sl these sts to a holder, work to end.

Rnd 25 Rep rnd 10, casting on 7 sts over sts on holder—34 sts. Work even in St st until piece measures 10½"/26.5cm from beg. Rep rnd 10 every rnd until 6 sts rem. Cut yarn, thread end through rem sts and pull closed.

Thumb shaping

With MC, k 7 sts from holder, pick up and k 7 sts across cast-on sts of thumb opening—14 sts. Divide sts over 3 dpns. Work in St st for 2"/5cm. Dec 4 sts evenly on each of next 2 rnds—6 sts. Cut yarn, thread end through rem sts and pull closed.

HAT

With dpn and MC, cast on 83 sts, divided over 3 dpns. Join to work in rnds. Pm for beg of rnd. P 3 rnds. K 12 rnds. P 3 rnds. Work in St st until piece measures 4¾"/12cm from beg.

Next (dec) rnd [K26, k2tog] twice, k27—81 sts.

Next (dec) rnd [K25, k2tog] twice, k27—79 sts. Work 6 more dec rnds, working 1 fewer st before decs each rnd—67 sts. P 3 rnds. K 1 rnd, dec 2 sts evenly—65 sts.

Crown shaping

Rnd 1 *K12, p1; rep from * around.

Rnd 2 *K2tog, k8, ssk, p1; rep from * around—55 sts.

Rnd 3 Knit.

Rnd 4 *K2tog, k6, ssk, p1; rep from * around—45 sts.

Rnds 5 and 6 Knit.

Rnds 7 and 9 Work as for rnd 4, working 1 fewer st between decs each rnd—25 sts.

Rnds 8 and 10 Knit.

Rnd 11 *K2tog, ssk, p1; rep from * around—15 sts. Cut yarn, thread end through rem sts and pull closed.

FULLING

Turn hat and mittens to WS. With tapestry needle, sew edges of purl ridges to form welt on RS. Wash pieces in same way as swatch. After washing, pull into shape and allow to dry flat.

FINISHING

Brush pieces with stiff brush to raise nap. With CC, make 38 2"/5cm pom-poms (see page 145). Sew 11 pom-poms around wrist of each mitten and 16 pom-poms around edge of hat. With CC, make a 3"/7.5cm tassel and attach to center top of hat. Foll diagram, work embroidery with *Tapestry (Princess)* yarn. ✣

EMBROIDERY DIAGRAM (HAT)

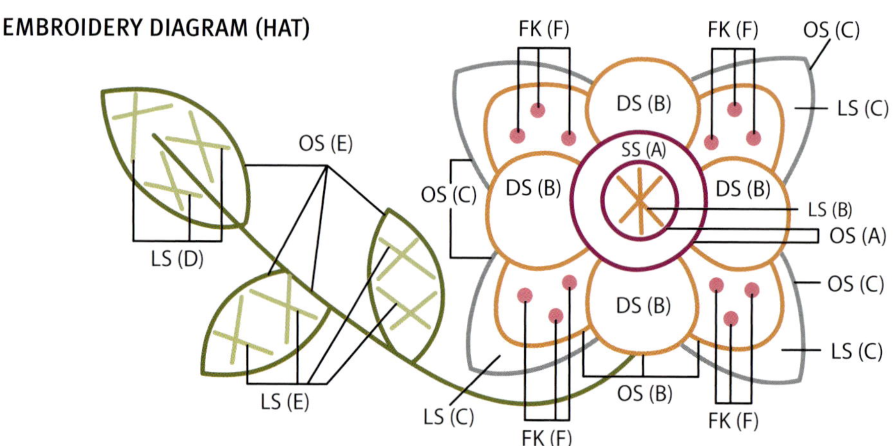

EMBROIDERY DIAGRAM (MITTENS)

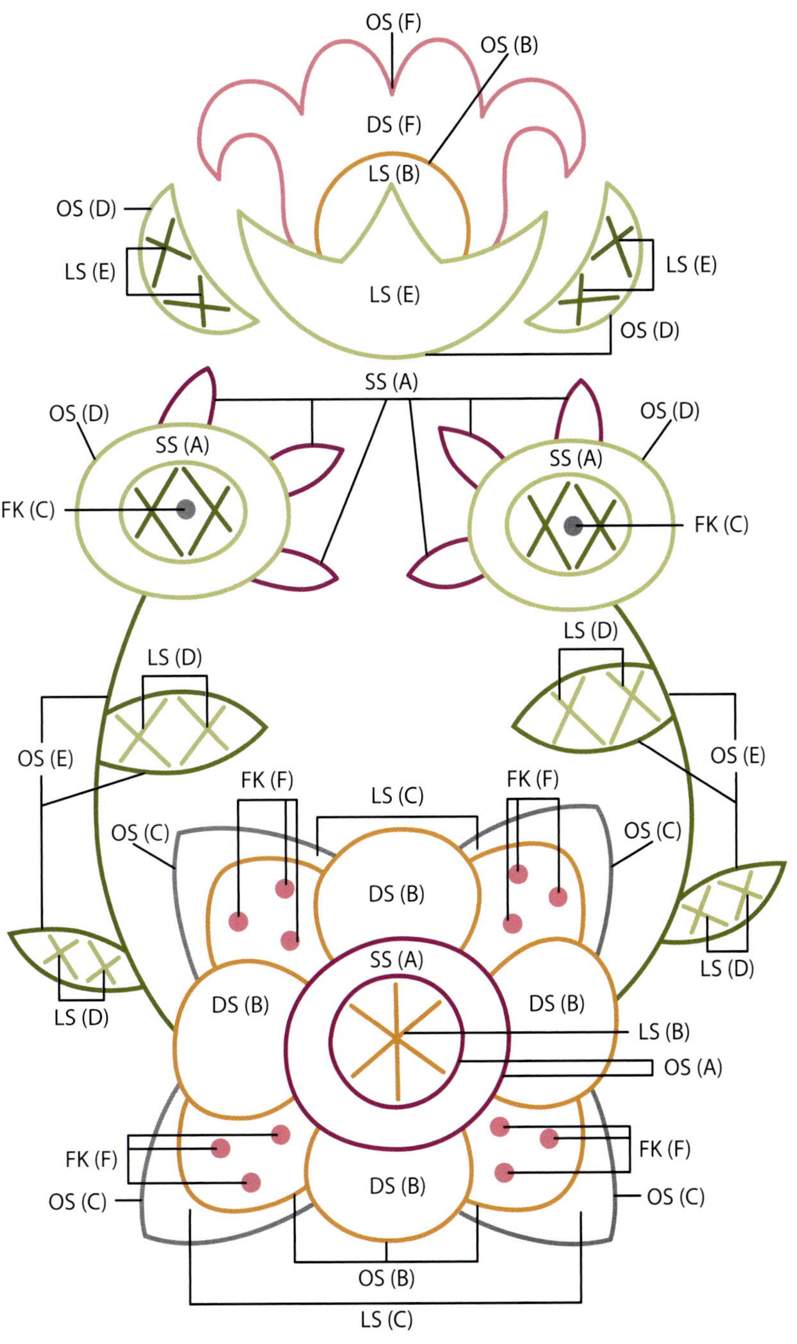

COLOR KEY

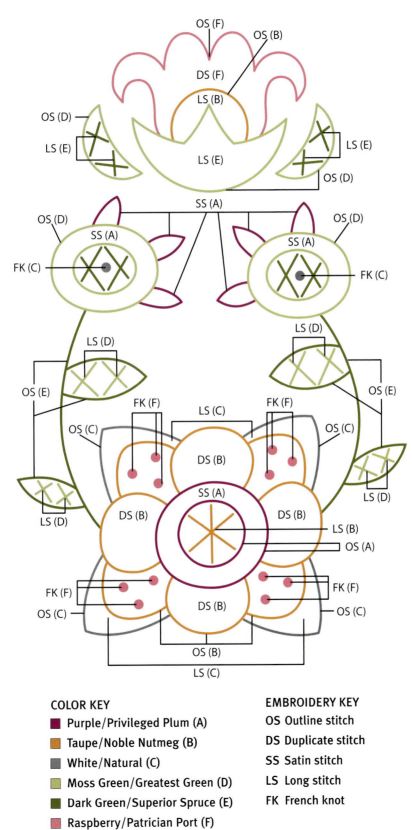

- Purple/Privileged Plum (A)
- Taupe/Noble Nutmeg (B)
- White/Natural (C)
- Moss Green/Greatest Green (D)
- Dark Green/Superior Spruce (E)
- Raspberry/Patrician Port (F)

EMBROIDERY KEY

OS Outline stitch
DS Duplicate stitch
SS Satin stitch
LS Long stitch
FK French knot

Glove-ly &

From dainty matinee gloves to graceful gauntlets to ultra-chic opera-length gloves, these designs go to great lengths to achieve gorgeous style.

Amazing

page 57

Expanding Cable Gloves

Opera-length gloves by Elli Stubenrauch feature an hourglass cable motif that expands as it runs up to the elbow. Knit from the fingers up, these beauties are shaped for an elegantly tailored fit.

KNITTED MEASUREMENTS

Hand circumference 7¼"/18.5cm

Length (from wrist to cuff) 12¾"/32.5cm

SIZE

Sized for adult woman.

MATERIALS

3 1¾oz/50g hanks (each approx 185yd/169m) of Louet North America *Gems Fingering* (superwash merino wool) in #90 paisley (1)

2 sets of 5 size 1 (2.25mm) double-pointed needles (dpns) OR SIZE TO OBTAIN GAUGE

Cable needle (cn)

Stitch markers

Tapestry needle

GAUGE

32 sts and 49 rnds = 4"/10cm over St st using size 1 (2.25mm) needles.

TAKE TIME TO CHECK GAUGE.

K1, P1 TUBULAR BIND-OFF

1) Cut the yarn 3 times the width of the ribbing and thread through tapestry needle. Insert tapestry needle purlwise into the first (knit) st, pull yarn through. Hold tapestry needle behind the knit st, insert it knitwise into the next purl st, pull yarn through.

2) *Sl first knit st knitwise onto tapestry needle, then insert tapestry needle into next knit st purlwise. Pull yarn through.

3) Sl the first st purlwise onto tapestry needle. Hold tapestry needle behind the knit st, insert it knitwise into the next purl st, pull yarn through. Rep from * until all sts are bound off.

STITCH GLOSSARY

2-st RC Sl 1 to cn, hold to *back,* k1 tbl, k1 from cn.

2-st LC Sl 1 to cn, hold to *front,* k1, k1 tbl from cn.

2-st RPC Sl 1 to cn, hold to *back,* k1 tbl, p1 from cn.

2-st LPC Sl 1 to cn, hold to *front,* p1, k1 tbl from cn.

3-st RC Sl 2 to cn, hold to *back,* k1 tbl, k2 from cn.

3-st LC Sl 1 to cn, hold to *front,* k2, k1 tbl from cn.

3-st RPC Sl 2 to cn, hold to *back,* k1 tbl, p2 from cn.

3-st LPC Sl 1 to cn, hold to *front,* p2, k1 tbl from cn.

3-st C Sl 1 to cn, hold to *back,* k1 tbl, move cn and hold to *front,* k1 tbl, k1 tbl from cn.

NOTES

1) Gloves are worked from fingertips to cuff with the first row worked flat, then joined for circular knitting on the foll rnd.

2) All five fingers are moved to spare dpns until they are needed.

RIGHT GLOVE

Thumb

With size 1 (2.5mm) dpn, cast on 4 sts.

Next (inc) row [K into front and back of a st (kfb)] 4 times—8 sts. Divide sts over 3 needles. Place marker (pm) and join, being careful not to twist.

Next (inc) rnd [Kfb] 8 times—16 sts.

Next (inc) rnd [Kfb, k3] 4 times—20 sts. K every

rnd until thumb measures 2"/5cm, or desired length. Break yarn, leaving 6"/15cm tail. Move these 20 sts to 2 spare dpns, dividing sts evenly between the 2 needles.

Little finger

Work as for thumb until there are 16 sts on needle. Work even until finger measures 2½"/6.5cm, or desired length. Break yarn, leaving 6"/15cm tail. Move these 16 sts to the same 2 spare dpns as thumb, dividing finger sts evenly between the 2 needles. Set aside.

Index finger

Work as for thumb until there are 16 sts on needle. **Next rnd** [Kfb, k7] twice—18 sts. Work even until finger measures 2¾"/7cm, or desired length. Break yarn, leaving 6"/15cm tail.

Move these 18 sts to 2 new spare dpns, dividing sts evenly between the 2 needles.

Middle finger

Work as for index finger until finger measures 3"/7.5cm, or desired length. Break yarn, leaving 6"/15cm tail. Move these 18 sts to the same dpns as index finger, dividing sts evenly between the 2 needles. The middle finger should be positioned to the right of the index finger, with the tails at the right edge of each finger.

Ring finger

Work as for index finger. Do not break yarn. Move these 18 sts to the same dpns as the index and middle fingers, dividing sts evenly between the 2 needles. The ring finger should be positioned to the right of the index and middle fingers, with the tails at the right edge of each finger.

Join first 3 fingers

(**Note** When resuming work on a finger, make sure the finger is oriented so that knitting continues at the same place work ceased on that particular rnd.)

Setup for joining fingers

(**Note** Be sure that fingers are arranged on 2 dpns from left to right as foll: index, middle, ring, with the working yarn at the right edge of the work.) There should be 27 sts on the front needle and 27 sts on the back needle—54 sts. Move 13 sts from the front needle to a 3rd dpn, and half of the sts from the back needle to a 4th dpn.

Join fingers

Next (dec and joining) rnd [K7, ssk, k2tog, k5, ssk, k2tog, k7] twice, pm—46 sts.

K 2 rnds.

Join little finger and thumb

Setup for joining little finger

Next rnd K44, ssk—45 sts. Move little finger sts to 2 spare dpns.

Join little finger

Work first 8 sts of little finger onto the end of the previous rnd as foll: K2tog, k6.

Next rnd Pm for new beg of rnd, k6, ssk, k2tog, k to end of rnd—58 sts. Divide sts evenly over 4 needles. Work even for 1"/2.5cm, or desired length from bottom of little finger to thumb join.

Setup for joining thumb

Next rnd K29, pm. Move thumb sts to 2 spare dpns.

Join thumb

Join 20 thumb sts as foll: K2tog, k16, ssk, pm, k to end of rnd—76 sts. Redistribute sts evenly over 4 needles. Work 2 rnds even.

Next (dec) rnd K to first marker, k2tog, k to 2 sts before next marker, ssk. Rep last 3 rnds 7 times more—60 sts. K 2 rnds, removing thumb markers.

Next (dec) rnd K28, ssk, k2tog, k28—58 sts.

Finish fingers

With tapestry needle and tails of fingers, sew the gaps between the fingers closed and weave in ends. (This will be more difficult to do when the arm is complete.)

Arm

Beg chart

(**Notes** 1) Chart only depicts the cabled half of the glove that runs along the top of the arm. The palm side of the glove is worked in St st with the same incs and decs as the cabled side. Foll the same chart for both sides, but omit the cable on the palm side. 2) The cables at each end of rnds 150 and 152 extend onto the palm side of the glove. On both rnds, the beg of the rnd is moved 1 st to the left to accommodate this.)

Rnd 1 Beg on palm side, work rnd 1 of chart over 29 sts (working decs and working k1 tbl as k1), pm, then for cable side, work chart rnd 1 over 29 sts—54 sts. Cont to foll chart as established (omitting cable on palm side) through chart rnd 149—74 sts.

Rnd 150 Remove rnd marker, k1, pm for new beg of rnd, k35, work rnd 150 of chart over 39 sts (removing 2nd marker).

Rnd 151 K35, work rnd 151 of chart over 39 sts.

Rnd 152 Remove rnd marker, k1, pm for new beg of rnd, k33, work rnd 152 of chart over 41 sts.

Rnd 153 K33, work rnd 153 of chart over 41 sts.

Rep last rnd 4 times more.

Ribbing

Next rnd *K1tbl, p1; rep from * to end of rnd.

Rep last rnd 9 times more.

FINISHING

Bind off, using k1, p1 tubular bind-off.

LEFT GLOVE

Work as for right glove, except beg rnds with cable side of glove and work palm side 2nd. ✣

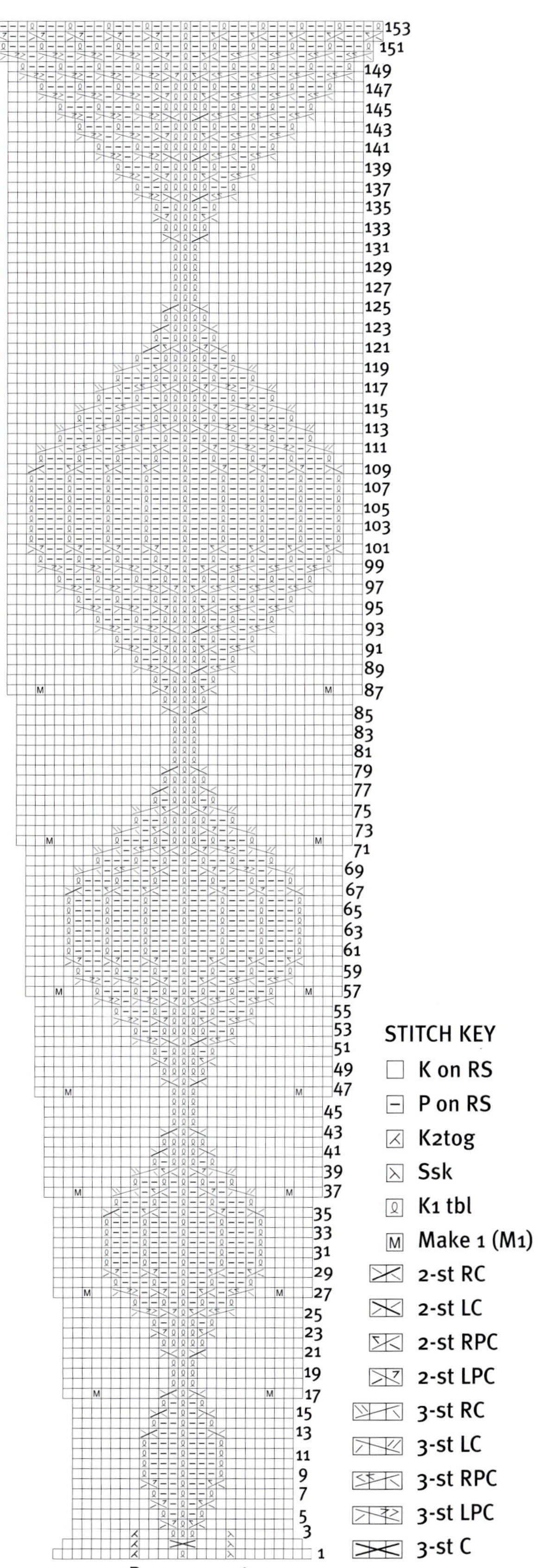

Autumn Leaves Gloves

Get your fingers ready for fall with leaf-motif gloves by Joanna Osborne and Sally Muir. The intarsia designs on the opera-length arms stand out against a black background.

KNITTED MEASUREMENTS

Hand circumference 7"/17.5cm

Length of cuff 13½"/34cm

SIZE

Sized for adult woman.

MATERIALS

2 1¾oz/50g balls (each approx 137yd/125m) of Lana Grossa/Muench Yarns *Pashmina* (extrafine merino wool/cashmere) in #8 black (MC) (4)

1 ball each in #13 dark charcoal (A), #30 medium charcoal (B), #24 navy (C), #12 taupe (D), #10 burgundy (E), #26 chocolate (F), #28 olive (G) and #25 eggplant (H)

One pair each sizes 3 and 5 (3.25 and 3.75mm) needles OR SIZE TO OBTAIN GAUGE

Two size 5 (3.75mm) double-pointed needles (dpns)

Stitch markers, bobbins and tapestry needle

GAUGE

24 sts and 32 rows = 4"/10cm over St st using larger needles.

TAKE TIME TO CHECK GAUGE.

NOTES

1) When changing colors, twist yarns on WS to prevent holes in work.

2) Use a separate bobbin for each color section. Do not carry yarn across back of work.

3) Gloves are worked back and forth in rows on straight needles. Dpns are used to work small number of sts in fingers.

K1, P1 RIB (over an odd number of sts)

Row 1 (RS) K1, *p1, k1; rep from * to end.

Row 2 P1, *k1, p1; rep from * to end.

Rep rows 1 and 2 for k1, p1 rib.

LEFT GLOVE

Cuff

With smaller straight needles and MC, cast on 45 sts. Work in k1, p1 rib for 8 rows, dec 1 st at beg of last row—44 sts. Change to larger straight needles. Cont in St st as foll:

Beg chart pat

Row 1 (RS) With MC, k14, place marker (pm), work chart pat over 30 sts.

Cont in pat as established through chart row 30.

Row 31 (dec row) With MC, k14, sl marker, work to last 2 sts of chart, k2tog—43 sts. Cont to dec 1 st at same edge on chart rows 61 and 91—41 sts. Work even through chart row 100. Remove marker. With MC only, cont as foll:

Thumb gusset

Inc row 1 (RS) K22, pm, M1, k1, M1, pm, k18—43 sts. Work 1 row even.

Inc row 2 (RS) K to first marker, sl marker, M1, k

to 2nd marker, M1, sl marker, k to end—45 sts. Rep inc row 2 every RS row 3 times more—51 sts. Work 3 rows even.

Thumb

Next row (RS) K33, turn, cast on 2 sts onto LH needle. Change to dpns.

Next row P13, including cast-on sts, turn, cast on 2 sts onto LH needle.

Next row K15, including cast-on sts—40 sts rem on straight needles.

Next row P15. Work even in St st over 15 sts for 2½"/6.5cm, end with a WS row.

Top shaping

Next (dec) row (RS) K1, [k2tog] 7 times—8 sts.

Next (dec) row [P2tog] 4 times—4 sts. Cut yarn, leaving an 8"/20.5cm tail. Thread through rem sts and cinch tightly to close.

Upper hand

Next row (RS) Return to sts on larger straight needles, join MC, pick up and k4 sts along cast-on sts of thumb, k to end—44 sts. Work even for 9 rows.

Index finger

Next row (RS) K28, turn, cast on 1 st onto LH needle. Change to dpns.

Next row P13, including cast-on st, turn, cast on 1 st onto LH needle.

Next row K14, including cast-on st—32 sts rem on straight needles.

Next row P14. Work even in St st over 14 sts for 3"/7.5cm, end with a WS row.

Top shaping

Next (dec) row (RS) [K2tog] 7 times—7 sts.

Next (dec) row P1, [p2tog] 3 times—4 sts. Complete as for thumb.

Middle finger

Next row (RS) Return to sts on larger straight needles, join MC, pick up and k2 sts along base of index finger, k5, turn, cast on 1 st onto LH needle. Change to dpns.

Next row P13, including cast-on st, turn, cast on 1 st onto LH needle.

Next row K14, including cast-on st—22 sts rem on straight needles.

Next row P14. Work even in St st over 14 sts for 3¼"/8cm, end with a WS row. Complete as for index finger.

Ring finger

Next row (RS) Return to sts on larger straight needles, join MC, pick up and k2 sts along base of middle finger, k5, turn, cast on 1 st onto LH needle. Change to dpns.

Next row P13, including cast-on st, turn, cast on 1 st onto LH needle.

Next row K14, including cast-on st—12 sts rem on straight needles.

Next row P14. Work even in St st over 14 sts for 3"/7.5cm, end with a WS row. Complete as for index finger.

Little finger

Next row (RS) Return to sts on larger straight needles, join MC, pick up and k2 sts along base of ring finger, k to end—14 sts. Change to dpns. Work even in St st for 2½"/6.5cm, end with a WS row. Cut a 20"/51cm long tail, complete as for index finger, then sew entire side seam.

RIGHT GLOVE

With smaller straight needles and MC, cast on 45 sts. Work in k1, p1 rib for 8 rows, dec 1 st at beg of last row—44 sts. Change to larger straight needles. Cont in St st as foll:

Beg chart pat

Row 1 (RS) Work chart pat over 30 sts, pm, with MC, k14.

Cont in pats as established through chart row 30.

Row 31 (dec row) K2tog, work chart to end, sl marker, with MC, k14—43 sts. Cont to dec 1 st at same edge on chart rows 61 and 91—41 sts. Work even through chart row 100. Remove marker. With MC only, cont as foll:

Thumb gusset

Inc row 1 (RS) K18, pm, M1, k1, M1, pm, k22—43 sts. Work 1 row even.

Inc row 2 (RS) K to first marker, sl marker, M1, k to 2nd marker, M1, sl marker, k to end—45 sts. Rep inc row 2 every RS row 3 times more—51 sts. Work 3 rows even. Complete as for left glove. ✣

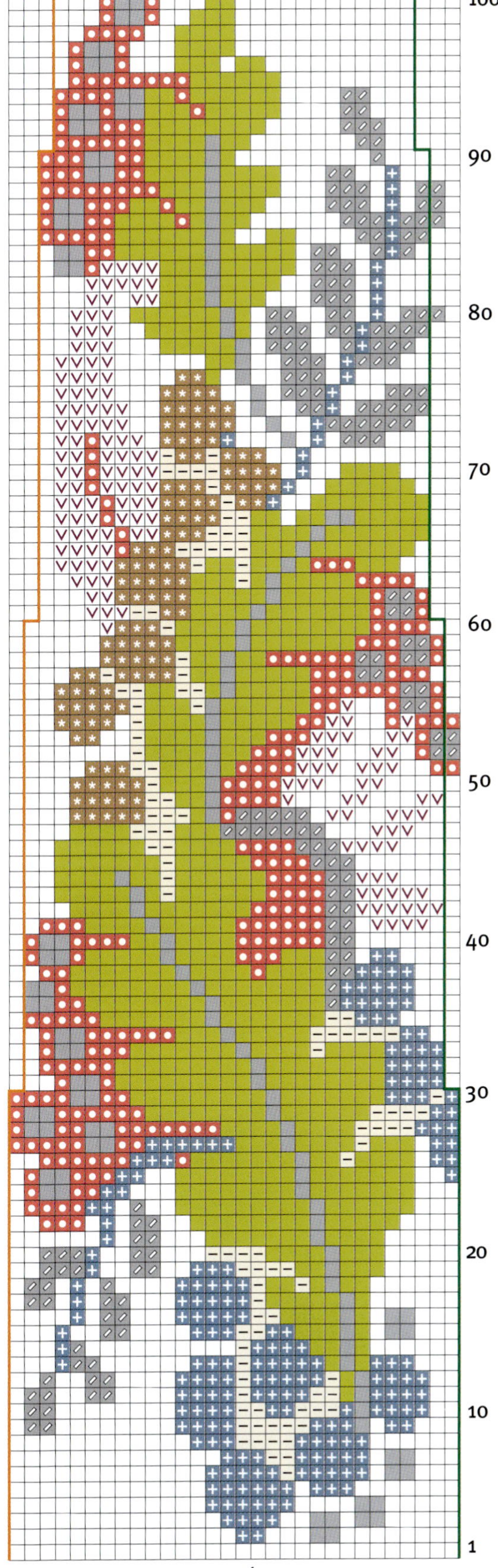

COLOR KEY

- Black (MC)
- Dark Charcoal (A)
- Medium Charcoal (B)
- Navy (C)
- Taupe (D)
- Burgundy (E)
- Chocolate (F)
- Olive (G)
- Eggplant (H)

GUIDES

- Right glove
- Left glove

Modern Aran Gauntlets and Hat

Challenging gauntlets by Deborah Newton, paired with a matching toque, are a fresh take on classic Aran knits. Featuring cables, bobbles and pom-poms, they're sure to leave Irish eyes smiling. First published in 1986, the set was updated with new yarn in 2007 for the *Vogue Knitting* twenty-fifth anniversary issue.

KNITTED MEASUREMENTS

Gloves

Circumference at cuff edge 14"/35.5cm

Circumference at lower edge 21"/53cm

Hat

Height 7½"/19cm

SIZE

Sized for adult woman.

MATERIALS

1986 yarn

Gloves 4 1¾oz/50g skeins (each approx 135yd/125m) of Berger du Nord *Douceur No. 4* (wool/mohair) in #8524 ecru (4)

Hat 6 1¾oz/50g balls (each approx 70yd/65m) of Berger du Nord *Douceur No. 5* (wool/mohair) in #8524 ecru (4)

2007 yarn

Gloves 4 1¾oz/50g balls (each approx 137yd/125m) of Knit One, Crochet Too, Inc *Ambrosia* (baby alpaca/silk/cashmere) in #510 pale moss (4)

Hat 4 1¾oz/50g balls (each approx 109yd/100m) of Knit One, Crochet Too, Inc. *Camelino* (merino/camel) in #510 pale moss (4)

Gloves: Set of 4 each sizes 4 and 5 (3.5 and 3.75mm) double-pointed needles (dpns)

Hat: Size 7 (4.5mm) circular needle, 16"/40cm long OR SIZE TO OBTAIN GAUGE

Hat: Set of 5 size 7 (4.5 mm) double-pointed needles (dpns) OR SIZE TO OBTAIN GAUGE

Cable needle (cn)

Stitch markers

GAUGES

Gloves 24 sts and 32 rows = 4"/10cm over St st using size 5 (3.75mm) needles and *Ambrosia.*

Hat 20 sts and 24 rows = 4"/10cm over St st using size 7 (4.5mm) needles and *Camelino.*

TAKE TIME TO CHECK GAUGES.

STITCH GLOSSARY

4-st RC Sl 2 to cn, hold to *back,* k2, k2 from cn.

4-st LC Sl 2 to cn, hold to *front,* k2, k2 from cn.

4-st RPC Sl 1 to cn, hold to *back,* k3, p1 from cn.

4-st LPC Sl 3 to cn, hold to *front,* p1, k3 from cn.

5-st RPC Sl 1 to cn, hold to *back,* k4, p1 from cn.

5-st LPC Sl 4 to cn, hold to *front,* p1, k4 from cn.

7-st RPC Sl 4 to cn, hold to *back,* k3, then p1, k3 from cn.

8-st RC Sl 4 to cn, hold to *back,* k4, k4 from cn.

8-st LC Sl 4 to cn, hold to *front,* k4, k4 from cn.

Make Bobble (MB) [K1, yo, k1, yo, k1] in a st—5 sts; turn, ssk, k1, k2tog; turn, p3; turn, S2KP.

MOCK CABLE PAT (over 2 sts)

Rnd 1 K2tog but leave sts on needle, insert RH needle between the 2 sts and k the first st again, sl both sts from needle.

Rnds 2, 3 and 4 K2.

Rep rnds 1–4 for mock cable pat.

LEFT GLOVE

With smaller dpns and *Ambrosia*, cast on 120 sts and divide evenly over 3 dpns. Place marker (pm) and join, taking care not to twist sts on needles.

Cuff edge

Foundation rnd [K2, p2] 10 times, pm, [k4, p4] twice, k4, p2, k4, [p4, k4] twice, pm, [p2, k2] 9 times, p2.

Beg chart pats

Rnd 1 [Work mock cable over 2 sts, p2] 10 times, [work chart 1 over 4 sts, p4] twice, work chart 1 over 4 sts, p2, [work chart 1 over 4 sts, p4] twice, work chart 1 over 4 sts, [p2, work mock cable over 2 sts] 9 times, p2.

Rnds 2–9 Cont in pats as established (working rnds 1–4 only of chart 1). Change to larger dpn.

Gauntlet/cuff

(**Note** Work chart 1 through rnd 6, then rep rnds 1–6.)

Rnd 10 Work 11 sts in pat, M1, work 20 sts in pat, M1, work to marker, work rnd 2 of chart 1 over 4 sts, M1, p4, k4, p4, k3, [k2tog] twice, k3, p4, k4, p4, M1, work rnd 2 of chart 1 over 4 sts, work 9 sts, M1, work 20 sts, M1, work to end—124 sts.

Rnd 11 Work mock cable over 2 sts, pm, p3, pm, work chart 3 over 13 sts, pm, p3, pm; rep from * once more, work rnd 3 of chart 1 over 4 sts, pm, p3, pm, work chart 4 over 28 sts, pm, p3, pm, work rnd 3 of chart 1 over 4 sts, pm, p3, pm, work chart 3 over 13 sts, pm, p3, pm, work mock cable over 2 sts, pm, p3, pm, work chart 3 over 13 sts, pm, p3. Cont in pats as established, working sts between chart pats in rev St st, AT SAME TIME, dec 1 st (by p2tog) in each p3-st section between chart pats every 16th rnd twice, then every 8th rnd once—94 sts. Work even through rnd 1 of 3rd rep of chart 4.

Wrist shaping

Next rnd [Work 2 sts mock cable, p3tog, k3tog, p1, k3tog tbl, p3tog tbl] twice, work rnd 4 of chart 1, work 28 sts in pat, work rnd 4 of chart 1, *p3tog, k3tog, p1, k3tog tbl, p3tog tbl*, work 2 sts mock cable, rep from * to * once more—62 sts.

Wrist ribbing

Change to smaller dpns.

Next rnd *Work 2 sts mock cable, [p1, k1] twice, p1; rep from * once more, work 4 sts chart 1, work rnd 3 of chart 4, work 4 sts chart 1, [p1, k1] twice, p1, work 2 sts mock cable [p1, k1] twice, p1.

Work 10 rnds in pats as established.

Next rnd Work 2 sts mock cable, *p1, k3, p1, work 2 sts mock cable, p1, k3, p1*, work 4 sts chart 1, work 28 sts chart 4, work 4 sts chart 1 rep from * to * once more. Change to larger dpns.

Hand

Work even in pats as established for 6 rnds more.

Thumb gusset

Next rnd Work through 2nd mock cable, p1, k1, pm, M1, k1, M1, pm (thumb sts), work to end of rnd—64 sts. Work 2 rnds even, knitting the M1's.

Next rnd Work to marker, M1, k3, M1, work to end of rnd—66 sts. Work 2 rnds even. Cont in this way to inc 2 sts inside of markers every 3 rnds until there are 15 sts between markers, end with rnd 15 of chart 4. Work 1 rnd even.

Thumb

(**Note** When measuring thumb and fingers, measure from cast-on sts. Measure your own fingers or try on gloves while knitting for best fit.)

Next rnd Work to thumb sts, k 15 sts and divide them onto 2 dpns, place all other sts on a holder. With 3rd dpn and same strand, cast on 5 sts. Join and place marker for beg of rnd.

K 2 rnds.

Next rnd K to 3rd needle, k2tog, k to end. Rep last 3 rnds 3 times more—16 sts. Work 4 rnds even.

Shape top

Change to smaller dpns.

Next rnd Knit.

Next rnd *K2tog; rep from * around. Rep last 2 rnds once more—4 sts. Fasten off by drawing yarn through rem sts, pull tightly and secure. Cont with hand as foll:

Next rnd With palm facing, sl sts from beg of rnd to thumb onto larger dpn, with new strand, pick up and k8 sts in 5 cast-on sts of thumb, work in pat to end of rnd—69 sts.

Next rnd [Work mock cable, p1, k3, p1] 3 times, work to end of rnd. Work even for 15 rnds more.

Next (dec) rnd [K2, k2tog, k1, ssk] twice, k2, k2tog, k2, p1, k2tog, k2, p2tog, k2tog, k2, p2tog, p2, k8, p3, k2tog, k2, p2tog, p1, ssk, k1, [ssk, k2] twice, k2tog, k1, ssk—53 sts. Discontinue all charts and cables. To work fingers, k the knit sts and p the purl sts.

Next rnd Work 26 sts, work 8-st LC over next 8 sts (center of back hand), work 11 sts, sl last 8 sts of rnd plus first 15 sts of rnd to dpn for palm sts, sl rem 30 sts to dpn for back of hand.

Index finger

Work to last 6 sts of palm, work these sts and place them on a separate dpn, work first 8 sts of back of hand on a 2nd dpn, sl rem 39 sts to holder. Cast on 3 sts on 3rd dpn. Join and place marker—17 sts. Work 3 rnds even.

Next rnd Work to p st, k2tog, work to end of rnd—16 sts. K every rnd until finger measures 1¼"/3cm. Dec 1 st at inner finger—15 sts. K every rnd until finger measures 2½"/6.5cm, or desired length. Shape top as for thumb.

Little finger

Sl first 5 sts of palm to separate dpn, sl last 8 sts of back of hand to 2nd dpn, cast on 2 sts on 3rd dpn. Join and place marker—15 sts. Work 1 rnd even.

Next rnd K2, ssk, work to end of rnd—14 sts. Work 2 rnds even.

Next rnd Work to p st, k2tog, work to end of rnd—13 sts. K every rnd until finger measures 1¼"/3cm. Dec 1 st at inner finger—12 sts. K every rnd until finger measures 1¾"/4.5cm, or desired length. Shape top as for thumb.

Ring finger

Sl next 6 sts of palm to separate dpn, sl next 7 sts of back of hand to 2nd dpn. Beg at palm, work 6 sts, cast on 3 sts, join and work across 7 sts of back of hand, pick up 2 sts in cast-on sts of little finger. Join and place marker—18 sts. Work 1 rnd even.

Next rnd K to last st of 3 cast-on sts, p next st, k3, ssk, work to end of rnd.

Next rnd Work to next p st, 5-st LPC, work to end. Work 5 rnds even.

Next rnd Work to last k st of 5-st LPC, ssk, work to end—16 sts. Work 2 rnds even.

Next rnd Work to 2nd p st, k2tog, work to end. Work 2 rnds even.

Next rnd Work to k st before p st, ssk, work to end. K every rnd until finger measures 2½"/6.5cm, or desired length. Shape top as for thumb.

Middle finger

Sl rem 6 sts of palm to separate dpn, sl rem 7 sts of back of hand to 2nd dpn. Beg at palm, work 6 sts, pick up 3 sts in cast-on sts of index finger, work across 7 sts of back of hand, pick up 2 sts in cast-on sts of ring finger. Join and place marker—18 sts.

Next rnd Work to first st of 2 cast-on sts, p next st, work to end of rnd.

Next rnd Work to p st before 4 k sts, k2tog, work to end.

Next rnd Work to p st before 4 k sts, 5-st RPC, work

to end. Work 5 rnds even.

Next rnd Work to first p st of 5-st RPC, k2tog, work to end—16 sts. Work 2 rnds even.

Next rnd Work to 2nd p st, k2tog, work to end. Work 2 rnds even.

Next rnd Work to p st, k2tog, work to end. K every rnd until finger measures 3"/7.5cm, or desired length. Shape top as for thumb.

RIGHT GLOVE

Work to correspond to left glove, reversing placement of pats, thumb and fingers. Make 4 twisted cords and 4 pom-poms. Attach pom-pom to one end of each cord and sew other end to side of wrist. Tie cords at back of hand through center cable twist of chart 4.

HAT

Vertical cable panels (make 3)

With straight needles and *Camelino*, cast on 46 sts.

Foundation row (RS) K1 (selvage st), p1, k4, pm, p3, pm, work row 24 of chart 4 over 28 sts, pm, p3, pm, k4, p1, k1 (selvage st).

Beg chart pats

Row 1 (WS) K2, work row 1 of chart 2 over 4 sts, k3, work row 1 of chart 4 over 28 sts, k3, work row 1 of chart 1 over 4 sts, k2. Cont in pats as established for 9 rows more.

Dec row (WS) Work in pat to first marker, sl marker, ssk, k1, sl marker, work in pat to next marker, sl marker, k2tog, k1, sl marker, work to end—44 sts. Cont to dec 1 st in p3-st sections every 12th row twice more, removing markers on last dec row—40 sts. Work even until row 1 of 3rd rep of chart 4 has been worked.

Next row (RS) *Bind off 2 sts, k2tog and bind off; rep from * to end.

Horizontal cable panel

With straight needles, cast on 46 sts.

Foundation row (RS) K1, [k4, p4] 5 times, k5.

Beg chart pats

Row 1 (WS) K1, *work row 1 of chart 2 over 4 sts, pm, k4, pm, work row 1 of chart 1 over 4 sts, pm, k4, pm; rep from * once more, work row 1 of chart 2 over 4 sts, pm, k4, pm, work row 1 of chart 1 over 4 sts, end k1.

Cont in pats as established until piece measures 2½"/6.5cm from beg, end with a WS row. Dec 1 st (by p2tog) in each p4-st section on next row—41 sts. Work even for 2"/5cm more, end with a WS row. Inc 1 st (by M1p) in each p4-st section—46 sts. Work even until piece measures 6½"/16.5cm from beg. Bind off.

Top of hat

With dpns, cast on 8 sts and divide evenly over 4 needles. Place marker and join, taking care not to twist sts.

(**Note** Keep the same number of sts on each needle. Instructions are written for one needle only, work rnds on each of 4 dpns.)

Rnd 1 K2 tbl.

Rnd 2 K into front and back of each st—4 sts.

Rnds 3–5 K1, p2, k1.

Rnd 6 M1p, k1, M1k, p2, M1k, k1, M1p—8 sts.

Rnds 7–11 P1, k2, p2, k2, p1.

Rnd 12 M1p, p1, M1k, k2, M1k, bring yarn to front of work over RH needle (not between needles) then to back again between needles (backward loop-BL), p2, BL, M1k, k2, M1k, p1, BL—16 sts.

Rnds 13–19 P2, work chart 1 over 4 sts, p4, work chart 2 over 4 sts, p2.

Rnd 20 [P1, M1p] twice, work 4 sts, [M1p, p1] 4 times, work 4 sts, [M1p, p1] twice—24 sts.

Rnds 21–24 P4, work 4 sts, p8, work 4 sts, p4.

Rnd 25 *[P2, M1p] twice, work 4 sts, [M1p, p2] twice, [p2, M1p] twice, work 4 sts, [M1p, p2] twice—32 sts.

Change to circular needle and work on all 128 sts as foll:

Rnd 26–28 [P6, work 4 sts, p12, work 4 sts, p6] 4 times.

Trim edging

Next rnd Cast on 3 sts onto LH needle, *k2, k2tog, sl 3 sts from RH needle to LH needle; rep from * until 3 sts rem on RH needle, sl 3 sts back to LH needle and bind off.

FINISHING

With cast-on edges at top, place 3 vertical cable panels side by side, sew tog, forming flat panel. With side edge at top, sew vertical cable panel to each end of flat panel, forming circle. Pin top of hat to top edge of panels, and sew in place so that trim edging extends slightly. With RS facing, pick up 1 st at center top of hat and MB.

Lower edging With RS facing and circular needle, pick up and k 24 sts along lower edge of each vertical panel, 32 sts along horizontal panel—104 sts. Cast on 3 sts onto LH needle, work same as trim edging. Make 3 twisted cords and 3 pom-poms and attach under bobble at top of hat. ✣

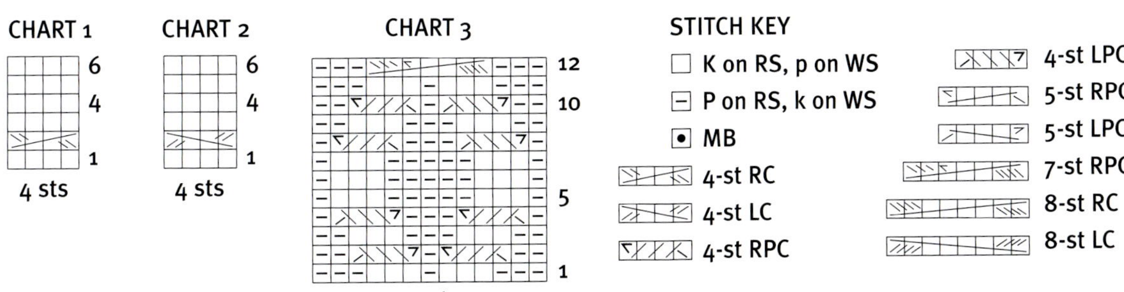

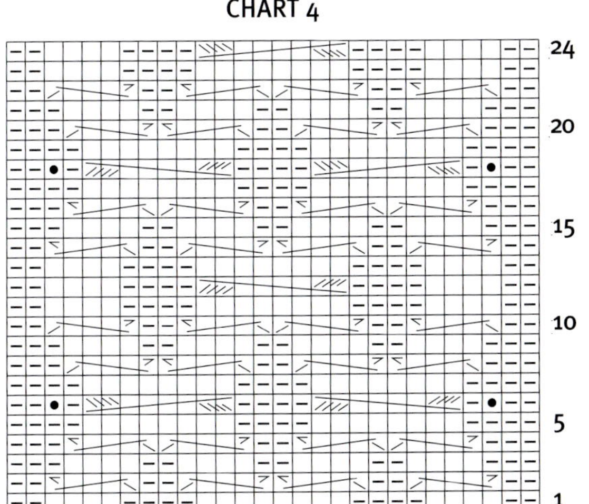

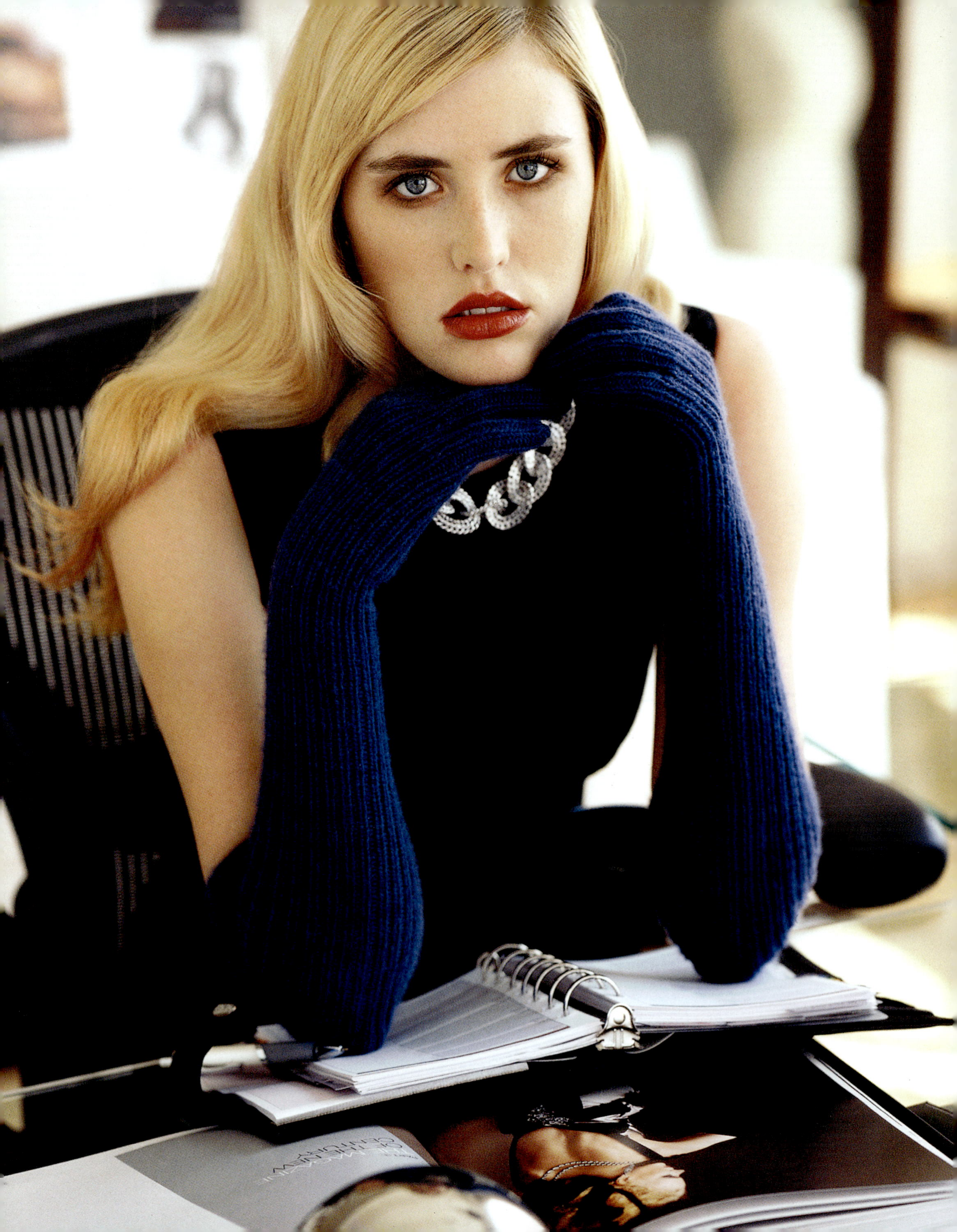

Ribbed Opera Gloves

Knit in a simple rib pattern and an elegant fiber, these above-the-elbow gloves by Anne Ryan are the height of understated elegance.

KNITTED MEASUREMENTS

Hand circumference 6½"/16.5cm

Length from middle finger to cuff 22½"/57cm

SIZE

Sized for Women's X-Small to Small.

MATERIALS

2 2oz/55g skeins (each approx 200yd/183m) of Jade Sapphire Exotic Fibres *4-Ply Mongolian Cashmere* (cashmere) in #20 lapis (4)

Set of 5 size 3 (3.25mm) double-pointed needles (dpns) OR SIZE TO OBTAIN GAUGE

Stitch markers and holders

GAUGE

32 sts and 30 rnds = 4"/10cm over k1, p1 rib (unstretched) using size 3 (3.25mm) needles.

TAKE TIME TO CHECK GAUGE.

GLOVES (make 2)

Cast on 48 sts and divide sts evenly over 4 dpns. Place marker and join, taking care not to twist sts.

Beg rib pat

Rnd 1 *K1, p1; rep from * around.

Rep rnd 1 until piece measure 6"/15cm from beg.

****Dec rnd** Ssk, rib to end—47 sts.

Next 2 rnds K2, p1, *k1, p1; rep from * to end.

Dec rnd Ssk, rib to end—46 sts. **

Work even in rib pat until piece measures 10"/25.5cm from beg.

Rep from ** to ** once more—44 sts.

Work even in rib pat until piece measures 14"/35.5cm from beg.

*****Inc rnd** K1, p1, M1, rib to last 2 sts, M1, k1, p1—46 sts.

Next 6 rnds K1, p1, k2, p1, *k1, p1; rep from * to last 3 sts, end k2, p1.

Inc rnd K1, p1, k1, M1p, *k1, p1; rep from * to last 3 sts, k1, M1p, k1, p1—48 sts. ***

Work 6 rnds even in rib pat.

Rep from *** to *** once more—52 sts.

Next rnd [K1, p1] twice, place the last 9 sts on holder (for thumb), *k1, p1; rep from * to holder, cast on 3 sts and join—46 sts.

Work 12 rnds even in rib pat.

Next rnd [K1, p1] 10 times, place last 8 sts on a holder (for little finger), *k1, p1; rep from * around—38 sts.

Next rnd [K1, p1] 10 times, cast on 2 sts and join, *k1, p1; rep from * around—40 sts.

Next rnd [K1, p1] 8 times, k1, p3, *k1, p1; rep from * to last 4 sts, ssk, k1, p1—39 sts.

Next rnd [K1, p1] 9 times, p2tog, *k1, p1; rep from * to last 3 sts, k2tog, p1—37 sts.

Next rnd [K1, p1] 9 times, k1, p2tog, *k1, p1; rep from * around—36 sts.

Next rnd [K1, p1] 12 times, place the last 12 sts on a holder (for ring finger), *k1, p1; rep from * around—24 sts.

Next rnd [K1, p1] 6 times, cast on 2 sts, *k1, p1; rep from * around—26 sts.

Next rnd [K1, p1] 6 times, p2, *k1, p1; rep from * around.

Next rnd [K1, p1] 6 times, p2tog, [k1, p1] 3 times, place last 13 sts on holder (for middle finger), *k1, p1; rep from * around—12 sts.

Index finger

Rnd 1 [K1, p1] 3 times, cast on 2 sts, *k1, p1; rep from * around—14 sts.

Rnd 2 [K1, p1] 3 times, p2, *k1, p1; rep from * around.

Rnd 3 [K1, p1] 3 times, p2tog, *k1, p1; rep from * around.

Rnd 4 [K1, p1] twice, k1, p2tog, *k1, p1; rep from * around—12 sts.

Work even in rib pat to desired length.

Next rnd *Ssk; rep from * around—6 sts.

Next rnd Knit. Cut yarn, leaving a 4"/10cm tail, thread through rem sts and pull tightly to cinch closed.

Middle finger

Place the 13 sts on the holder back on needles.

Rnd 1 [K1, p1] twice, k1, p2tog, *k1, p1; rep from * around, pick up and k 2 sts at base of index finger—14 sts.

Rnd 2 [K1, p1] 6 times, p2tog—13 sts.

Rnd 3 [K1, p1] 5 times, k1, p2tog—12 sts.

Work even in rib pat to desired length.

Complete as for middle finger.

Ring finger

Place the 12 sts on the holder back on needles, pick up and k 2 sts from the base of the middle finger—12 sts. Work as for middle finger.

Little finger

Place the 8 sts on the holder back onto the needles.

Rnd 1 *P1, k1; rep from * around, pick up and k 2 sts at base of ring finger—10 sts.

Work even in rib pat to desired length.

Next rnd *K2tog; rep from * around—5 sts.

Next rnd Knit. Cut yarn, leaving a 4"/10cm tail, thread through rem sts and pull tightly to cinch closed.

Thumb

Place the 9 sts on the holder back onto the needles.

Rnd 1 *P1, k1; rep from * around, end p1, pick up and k 5 sts at base of hand—14 sts.

Work even in rib pat to desired length.

Next rnd *K2tog; rep from * around—7 sts.

Next rnd Knit. Cut yarn, leaving a 4"/10cm tail, thread through rem sts and pull tightly to cinch closed. ✣

Embroidered Gauntlets

Nicky Epstein's showstopping gloves are knit in basic stockinette stitch to allow bright picot cuffs and delicate floral embroidery to take center stage.

KNITTED MEASUREMENTS

Circumference at upper arm 8¾ (9½)"/22 (24)cm

Circumference at wrist 7½ (8¼)"/19 (21) cm

Length to base of fingers 11½"/29cm

SIZE

Sized for Women's Small/Medium (Large/X-Large) and shown in size Small/Medium.

MATERIALS

3 1¾ oz/50g balls (each approx 176yd/160m) of Lana Grossa/Unicorn Books and Crafts *Cool Wool 2000* (wool) in #433 black (A) (2)

1 ball in #481 celery (B)

Small amounts in #466 lt blue, #437 tan, #482 rose, #483 plum and #439 purple for embroidery

Set of 4 size 3 (3.25mm) double-pointed needles (dpns)

Stitch marker

Tapestry needle

Scrap yarn

GAUGE

26 sts and 34 rnds = 4"/10cm over St st using size 3 (3.25mm) needles. TAKE TIME TO CHECK GAUGE.

RIGHT GLOVE

With B, cast on 57 (61) sts. Divide sts onto 3 dpns—19 (20) sts on 2 dpns, 19 (21) sts on 1 dpn. Place marker and join, taking care not to twist sts.

K 5 rnds.

Picot turning rnd K1, *yo, k2tog; rep from * around. K 5 rnds. Break B. Change to A. Cont in St st, dec 1 st at end of every 8th (10th) rnd (last 2 sts before marker) 9 (7) times—48 (54) sts.

Redistribute sts evenly over 3 dpns—16 (18) sts on each dpn.

Work even until piece measures 7"/18cm from picot rnd, or desired length to base of thumb.

Thumb gore

Rnd 1 K26 (29), p1, M1, k1, M1, p1, k19 (22)—50 (56) sts.

Rnds 2 and 3 K the knit sts and M1's and p the purl sts.

Rnd 4 K26 (29), p1, M1, k3, M1, p1, k19 (22)—52 (58) sts. Cont to inc 2 sts (by working M1 after first p1 and before 2nd p1) every 3rd rnd 5 times more—62 (68) sts. Work 3 rnds even.

Next rnd K27 (30), sl next 15 sts to scrap yarn and cast on 3 sts for inside edge of thumb, k20 (23)—50 (56) sts. Work even for 1¾"/4.5cm more, or desired length to base of fingers.

Index finger

K15 (18) and sl these sts to scrap yarn, k14 (16), cast on 2 sts for inner edge of finger and sl rem 21 (22) sts to other end of same yarn strand. Join and work in rnds on 16 (18) sts, redistributing sts on 3 dpns, until finger measures 3"/7.5cm, or ¼"/.5cm less than desired length.

Dec rnd [K2tog] 8 (9) times—8 (9) sts.

Next rnd Knit.

Dec rnd [K1, k2tog] 2 (3) times, k2 (0)—6 sts.

Next rnd [K2tog] 3 times—3 sts. Cut yarn and draw through rem sts to close.

Middle finger

Sl 5 (6) sts from back of hand to dpn, k these sts, then pick up and k 2 sts at base of index finger, k7 (8) sts from palm of hand, cast on 2 sts at end—16 (18) sts. Complete as for index finger, working until finger measures 3½"/9cm.

Ring finger

Work as for middle finger, working until finger measures 3¼"/8.5cm.

Little finger

Sl 6 sts from back of hand to dpn, k these sts, then pick up and k 2 sts at base of ring finger, k rem 6 sts—14 sts. Work until finger measures 2½"/6.5cm.

Dec rnd [K2tog] 7 times—7 sts.

Next rnd Knit.

Dec rnd [K2tog] 3 times, k1—4 sts. Cut yarn and draw through rem sts to close.

Thumb

Place 15 sts of thumb onto 2 dpns.

Rnd 1 K15, then with 3rd dpn, pick up and k 3 sts at base of thumb—18 sts. Cont in rnds until thumb measures 2¾"/7cm. Complete as for larger size of index finger.

LEFT GLOVE

Work as for right glove to thumb gore.

Thumb gore

Rnd 1 K19 (22), p1, M1, k1, M1, p1, k26 (29). Cont as for right glove to index finger.

Index finger

K21 (22) and sl to scrap yarn, k16, cast on 2 sts for inner edge of finger, sl rem 15 (18) sts to other end of same yarn strand. Complete as for right glove.

FINISHING

Block gloves lightly. Fold picot hem to WS and sew in place. Using photo as guide for colors, embroider motifs on front of hand, foll diagram and illustrations on page 143. ✣

EMBROIDERY DIAGRAM

Leaf-Lace Gloves

With a leaf-lace panel adorning the back of the hand, these cashmere-blend gloves are perfect for fall. Lisa Hoffman offsets the lace with a ribbed cuff to keep wrists insulated from autumn's chill.

KNITTED MEASUREMENTS

Circumference (back of hand above thumb)
7½"–8"/19cm–20.5cm
Length (tip of middle finger to bottom of cuff)
11½"/29cm

SIZE

Sized for adult woman.

MATERIALS

2 1¾oz/50g hanks (each approx 160yd/146m) of Artyarns *Cashmere Sock* (cashmere/wool/nylon) in #295 oxblood (2)
Set of 4 size 2 (2.75mm) double-pointed needles (dpns) OR SIZE TO OBTAIN GAUGE
One pair size 2 (2.75mm) needles
2 spare size 2 (2.75mm) dpns to hold sts when working fingers
Scrap yarn (for cast-on)
Stitch markers
Tapestry needle

GAUGE

28 sts and 36 rnds = 4"/10cm over St st, using size 2 (2.75mm) needles.
TAKE TIME TO CHECK GAUGE.

STITCH GLOSSARY

M1R Insert LH needle from back to front under strand between last st worked and next st on LH needle. K into front loop to twist st.
M1L Insert LH needle from front to back under strand between last st worked and next st on LH needle. K into back loop to twist st.

K3, P3 RIB (over a multiple of 6 sts)

Rnd 1 *K3, p3; rep from * around.
Rep rnd 1 for k3, p3 rib.

LEFT GLOVE

With straight needles and scrap yarn, cast on 27 sts using double (or long tail) cast-on method. Change to main yarn. Beg with a knit row, work 3 rows in St st (k on RS, p on WS).
Next row (WS) *P1, k1 from first row by inserting LH needle from back to front into the bump of the st peeking through scrap yarn and k1 tbl; rep from * to end—54 sts.
Remove scrap yarn. Divide sts evenly over 3 dpns. Place marker (pm) and join, being careful not to twist sts.

Cuff

Work in k3, p3 rib for 4"/10cm.

Hand

Beg lace chart

Rnd 1 K15, p3, work rnd 1 of lace chart over 15 sts, p3, k18. Cont in pat as established until 8 rnds of chart have been worked twice.

Thumb gusset

Next (inc) rnd K10, pm, M1L, k2, M1R, pm, k3, p3,

work chart pat over 15 sts, p3, k18—56 sts. Rep inc rnd every other rnd 8 times more—72 sts.

Next rnd K10, place 20 thumb sts on scrap yarn (removing markers), work in pat to end of rnd—52 sts. Cont in pat until piece measures approx 8"/20.5cm, or desired length, to base of fingers, end with chart rnd 8.

Next rnd Remove rnd marker, k11, pm for new beg of rnd.

Little finger

Next rnd K20 and place these sts on spare dpn. With free needle, k6, with 2nd needle, k6, with 3rd needle, cast on 3 sts, place rem 20 sts on spare dpn—15 little finger sts, 40 sts on spare dpns. Divide 15 finger sts evenly over needles and k every rnd for 2"/5cm, or desired length.

Next (dec) rnd [Ssk, k1, ssk] 3 times—9 sts.

Next (dec) rnd [Ssk, k1] 3 times—6 sts. Cut yarn and thread through rem sts with tapestry needle. Cinch closed.

Ring finger

Place next 6 sts from each spare dpn onto 2 working dpns. Rejoin yarn at palm-side base of previous finger. With free needle, k6, with 2nd needle, cast on 3 sts, with 3rd needle, k6, pick up and k 2 sts from cast-on sts of previous finger—17 sts.

Join, distributing sts evenly on needles, and k every rnd for 3"/7.5cm, or desired length.

Next (dec) rnd [Ssk, k1, ssk] 3 times, ssk—10 sts.

Next (dec) rnd [Ssk, k1] twice, [ssk] twice—6 sts. Cut yarn and thread through rem sts with tapestry needle. Cinch closed.

Middle finger

Place next 7 sts from each spare dpn onto 2 working needles. Rejoin yarn at palm-side base of previous finger.

With free needle, k5, with 2nd needle, k2, cast on 1 st, k2, with 3rd needle, k5, pick up and k 2 sts from cast-on sts of previous finger—17 sts. Join, distributing sts evenly on needles, and k every rnd for 3¼"/8.5cm, or desired length. Work dec rnds same as for ring finger.

Index finger

Work as for middle finger for 3"/7.5cm, or desired length. Work dec rnds same as for ring finger.

Thumb

Place 20 sts from scrap yarn on 3 dpns. Rejoin yarn at palm-side.

Next rnd K19, k last st of rnd tog with first st of next rnd—19 sts. K every rnd for 2"/5cm, or desired length.

Next rnd [Ssk, k1] 5 times, [ssk] twice—12 sts.

Next rnd [Ssk] 6 times—6 sts. Cut yarn and pull through rem sts.

RIGHT GLOVE

Work as for left glove until cuff measures 4"/10cm.

Hand

Beg lace chart

Rnd 1 K18, p3, work rnd 1 of lace chart over 15

sts, p3, k15. Cont in pat until 8 rnds of lace chart have been worked twice.

Thumb gusset

Next (inc) rnd K18, p3, work lace chart over 15 sts, p3, k3, pm, M1L, k2, M1R, pm, k10. Rep inc rnd every other rnd 8 times more—72 sts.

Next rnd Work to first marker, place 20 thumb sts on scrap yarn (removing markers), work to end of rnd—52 sts. Work even until glove measures 8"/20.5cm, or desired length to base of fingers, end with chart rnd 7.

Next rnd Drop rnd marker, work to last 11 sts, pm for new beg of rnd.

Little finger

Next rnd K20 and place these sts on spare dpn. With free needle, k6, with 2nd needle, k6, with 3rd needle, cast on 3 sts, place rem 20 sts on spare dpn—15 finger sts, 40 sts on spare dpns. Join 15 finger sts, divided evenly over needles, and work as for left glove.

Work rem fingers and thumb as for left glove, only rejoining yarn at back of hand.✣

LACE CHART

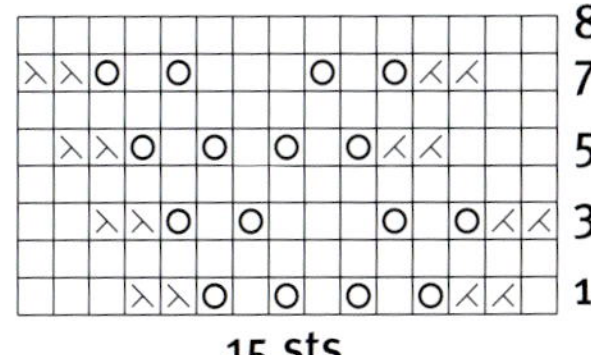

STITCH KEY

- ☐ K on RS
- ⊡ Yo
- ⧄ K2tog
- ⧅ Ssk

Riding Gloves

You'll jockey for a chance to wear these equestrian-inspired gloves by Nicole Egaña.

KNITTED MEASUREMENTS

Hand circumference 7"/18cm

SIZE Sized for adult woman.

MATERIALS

1 1¾ oz/50g skein (approx 175yd/160m) each of Koigu Wool Designs *KPM* (merino wool) in #2229 red (A) and #2400 black (B) (1)

One pair size 2 (2.75mm) needles OR SIZE TO OBTAIN GAUGE

Set of 5 size 2 (2.75mm) double-pointed needles

Stitch markers and holders

GAUGE

28 sts and 44 rows = 4"/10cm over St st.

TAKE TIME TO CHECK GAUGE

WRISTBANDS (make 2)

With B, cast on 6 sts. Work in St st for 7"/18cm, end with a WS row.

Buttonhole row (RS) K2, bind off 2 sts, k to end.

Next row (WS) P2, cast on 2 sts, p to end. Work 10 rows more in St st. Bind off.

RIGHT GLOVE

With A and RS facing, pick up and k 42 sts along side edge of wristband, beg 2 rows from buttonhole, and ending 12 rows before end of band.

Row 1 (WS) K3, p36, k3.

Row 2 (RS) Knit.

Rep rows 1 and 2 once more, then row 1 once more.

Thumb gusset

Next (inc) row (RS) K10, place marker (pm), M1, k1, M1, pm, k to end—44 sts.

Next row (WS) K3, p to last 3 sts, k3.

Next (inc) row K to marker, sl marker, M1, k to next marker, M1, sl marker, k to end—46 sts.

Rep last 2 rows once more, then work 1 more WS row—48 sts.

Next (RS) row Cast on 1 st to LH needle, k this st, then work inc row—51 sts.

Next (WS) row Cast on 1 st to LH needle, k this st, k3, p to last 4 sts, k4—52 sts. Cont in this way to cast on 1 st at beg of next 2 rows, working cast-on sts in garter st—56 sts.

***Next (RS) row** Cast on 5 sts to LH needle, k these sts, then work inc row to last 8 sts, pm for beg of next rnd, k to end of row—63 sts. Distribute all sts on 4 dpns, keeping 3 markers in place, and join to work in the round at the beg-of-rnd marker.

Next rnd K3, p15, k45.

Next (inc) rnd K around, working as inc row—65 sts.

Rep last 2 rnds once more, keeping 15 garter sts as established—67 sts.

Next rnd K to first thumb gusset marker, place the 17 thumb gusset sts on holder to be worked later, cast on 1 st to LH needle, k this st, k to end of rnd—51 sts. Work in St st until glove measures 3½"/9cm above wristband.

Little finger

Next rnd K first 6 sts, place next 40 sts on a holder, cast 1 st onto LH needle and k this st, k rem 5 sts—12 sts. Distribute these 12 sts on 4 dpns, pm and join. Work in St st until finger measures 2¼"/5.5cm, or desired length.

Next (dec) rnd *K2tog; rep from * to marker—6 sts. Cut yarn, leaving a long tail, thread through rem sts, cinch tightly to close.

Ring finger

Place next 7 sts each from back of hand and palm on dpn, cast on 2 sts over gap between ring finger and middle finger—16 sts. Distribute sts evenly over 4 dpns, pm and join. Work in St st until finger measures 2½"/6.5cm, or desired length.

Next (dec) row *K2tog; rep from * to marker—8 sts. Finish as for little finger.

Middle finger

Place next 6 sts each from back of hand and palm on dpns, pick up and k 2 sts from edge of ring finger, cast on 2 sts over gap between ring finger and middle finger—16 sts. Distribute sts evenly over 4 dpns, pm and join. Work in St st until finger measures 2¾"/7cm, or desired length.

Next (dec) row *K2tog; rep from * to marker—8 sts. Finish as for little finger.

Index finger

Distribute rem 14 sts over 4 dpns, pick up and k 2 sts along edge of middle finger—16 sts. Pm and join. Work in St st until finger measures 2½"/6.5cm, or desired length.

Next (dec) row *K2tog; rep from * to marker—8 sts. Finish as for little finger.

Thumb

Place 17 sts from holder on dpns, pick up and k 1 st along edge between thumb and hand. Arrange 18 sts evenly over 4 dpns, pm and join. Work in St st until thumb measures 2¼"/5cm, or desired length.

Next (dec) row *K2tog; rep from * to marker—9 sts. Finish as for little finger.

LEFT GLOVE

Work as for right glove to thumb gusset.

Next (inc) row K31, pm, M1, k1, M1, pm, k10—44 sts.

Next row (WS) K3, p to last 3 sts, k3.

Work as for right glove to *.

Next (RS) row Cast on 5 sts to LH needle, k these sts, k8, pm for beg of next rnd, then work inc row—63 sts. Distribute all sts on 4 dpns, keeping 3 markers in place, and join to work in the round at the beg-of-rnd marker.

Next rnd K45, p15, k3.

Next (inc) rnd K around, working as inc row—65 sts. Rep last 2 rnds once more, keeping 15 garter sts as established—67 sts.

Next rnd K to first thumb gusset marker, place the 17 thumb gusset sts on holder to be worked later, cast on 1 st to LH needle, k this st, k to end of rnd—51 sts. Work in St st until glove measures 3½"/9cm above wristband.

Little finger

Next rnd K first 5 sts, place next 40 sts on a holder, cast 1 st onto LH needle and k this st, k rem 6 sts—12 sts. Distribute these 12 sts on 4 dpns, pm and join. Work as for little finger on right glove. Work rem fingers and thumb in same manner as right glove.

I-CORD

With B, cast on 3 sts. *Without turning work, starting on left side of the keyhole of glove, pick up the first st in St st after garter st border. Without turning work, k2tog, k2. Rep from * around the edge of the keyhole to wristband. Cut yarn, leaving a long tail, thread through sts, cinch tightly to close, thread yarn through to back side of glove. Rep for 2nd glove.

FINISHING

Turn gloves inside out, weave in ends. ✣

Cabled-Cuff Gloves

These loose-fitting gloves, designed by Michele Rose Orne, have a tight hold on style. Start flat at the cabled cuffs, which button closed, and move into the round as you make your way up the hand.

KNITTED MEASUREMENTS

Hand circumference 8½"/21.5cm

Length of cuff 5½"/14cm

SIZE

Sized for Women's Large. (For a smaller-fitting glove, use needles 1 size smaller than the recommended needles, beg on rnd 43.)

MATERIALS

2 1¾oz/50g hanks (each approx 125yd/114m) of Alchemy Yarns of Transformation *Sanctuary* (wool/silk) in #91m copper (3)

Set of 5 size 4 (3.5mm) double-pointed needles (dpns) OR SIZE TO OBTAIN GAUGE

Cable needle (cn)

Stitch markers

Two ⅜"/10mm ball buttons

GAUGE

26 sts and 32 rows = 4"/10cm over St st using size 4 (3.5mm) needles.

TAKE TIME TO CHECK GAUGE.

STITCH GLOSSARY

2-st RT Sl 1 to cn, hold to *back,* k1, k1 from cn.

2-st LT Sl 1 to cn, hold to *front,* k1, k1 from cn.

2-st RPT Sl 1 to cn, hold to *back,* k1, p1 from cn.

2-st LPT Sl 1 to cn, hold to *front,* p1, k1 from cn.

4-st LC Sl 2 to cn, hold to *front,* k2, k2 from cn.

3-st RPC Sl 1 to cn, hold to *back,* k2, p1 from cn.

3-st LPC Sl 2 to cn, hold to *front,* p1, k2 from cn.

Make Bobble (MB) [K1, p1, k1] into 1 st, turn. P3, turn. K3, turn. P3, turn. SK2P.

RIGHT GLOVE

Cuff strip

Cast on 6 sts. Using 2 needles and working back and forth in rows, work as foll:

Rows 1 and 3 (RS) Knit.

Rows 2 and 4 Purl.

Row 5 4-st RC, k2.

Row 6 Purl.

RIGHT GLOVE

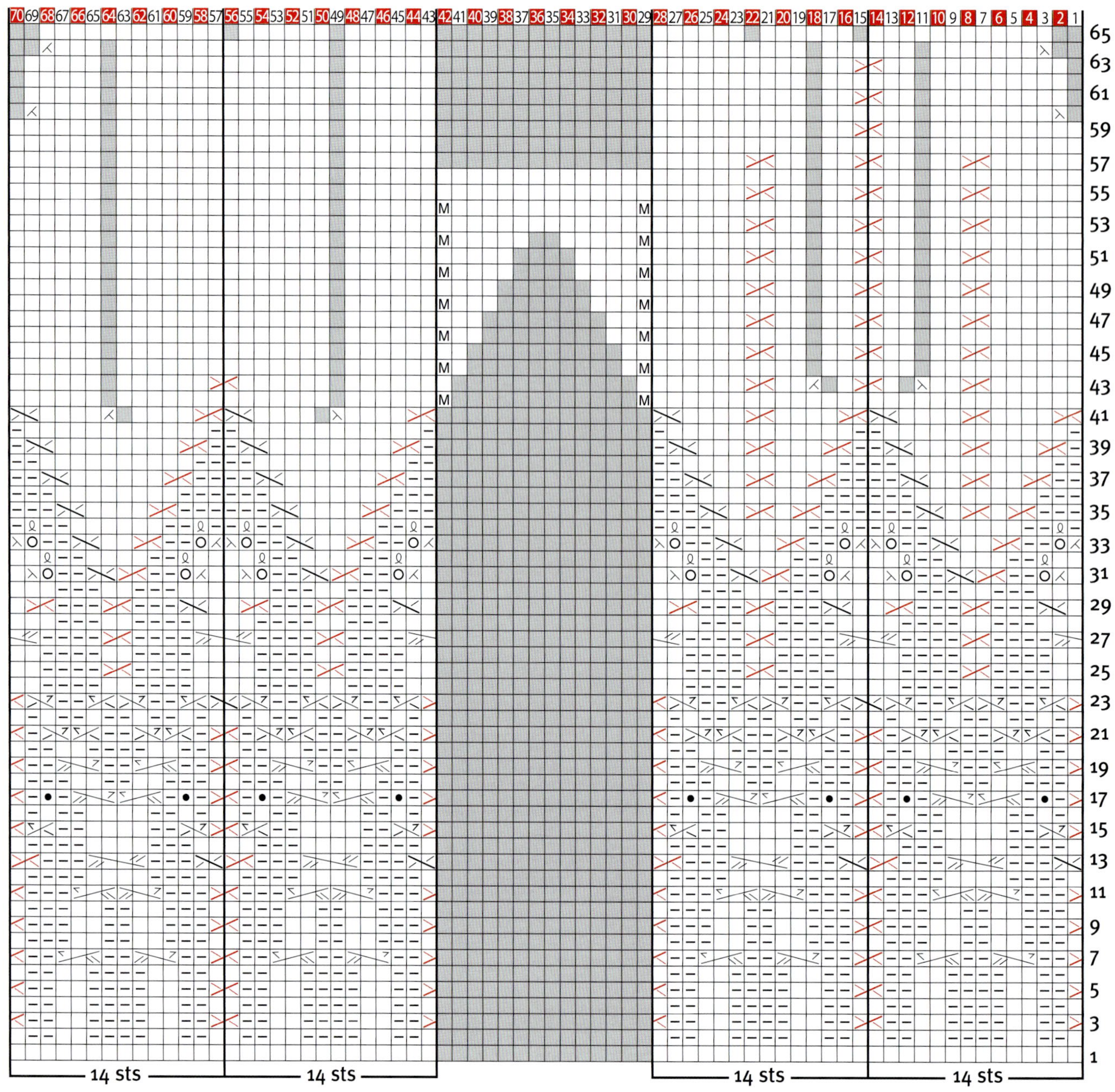

STITCH KEY

- K on RS, p on WS
- P on RS, k on WS
- Yo
- K1 tbl
- No stitch
- MB
- M1
- K2tog
- Ssk
- or 2-st RT
- or 2-st LT
- 2-st RPT
- 2-st LPT
- 3-st RPC
- 3-st LPC
- 4-st LC
- or 4-st LC

LEFT GLOVE

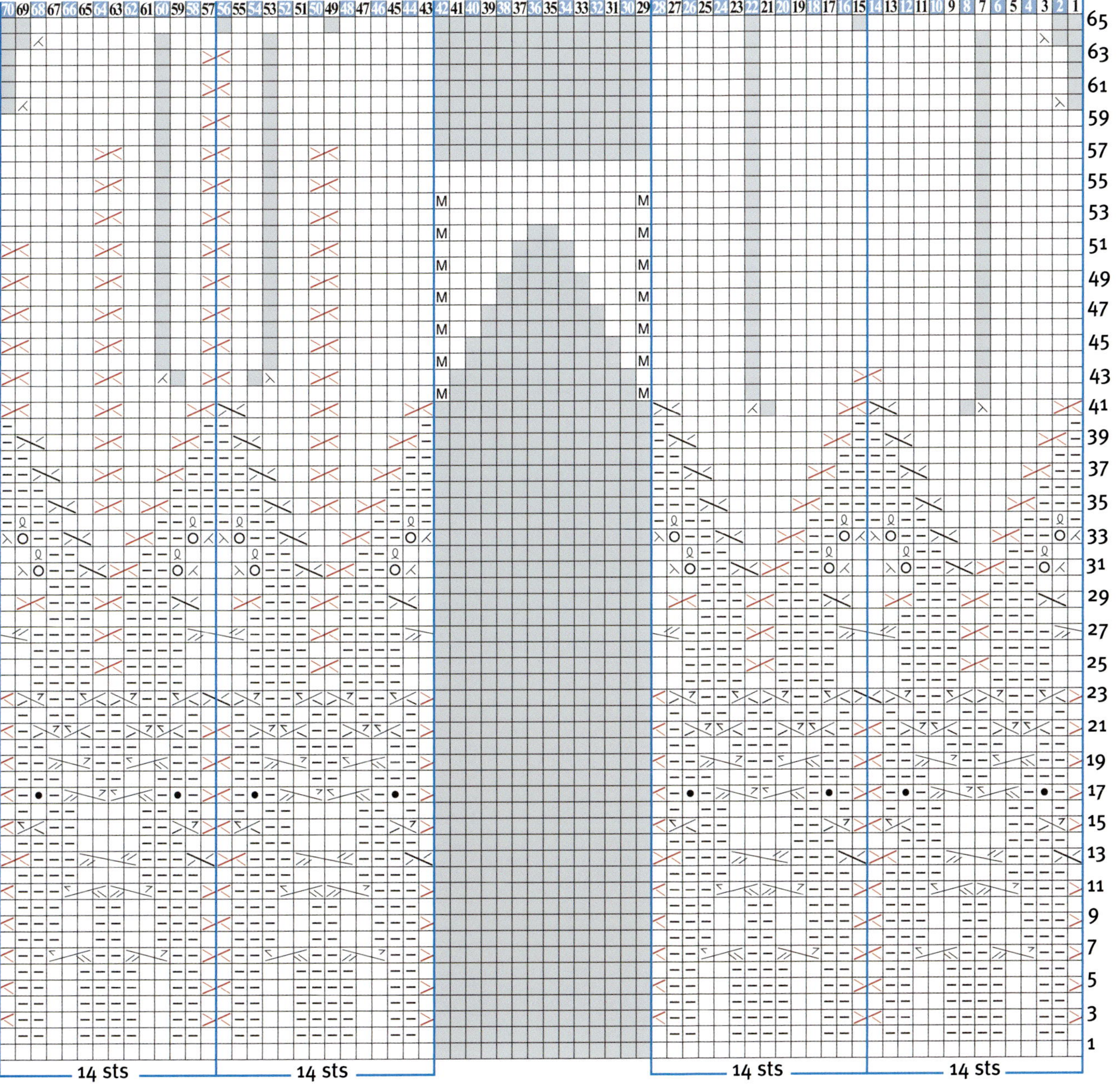

Rep rows 1–6 until cuff measures 7"/18cm from beg, end with a WS row.

Buttonhole row (RS) K2, bind off 2 sts, k 1 more.

Next row Purl, casting on 2 sts over the bound-off sts.

K 1 row, p 1 row. Bind off.

Cuff

Turn the cuff strip sideways and with cable at the lower edge, pick up and k 56 sts from the opposite edge, ending at the center of the buttonhole (leave this last ½"/1.5cm of strip free). Divide sts onto 4 dpns with 14 sts on each dpn (note that chart is divided into 4 sets of 14 sts each). Join and pm to mark beg of rnd.

Beg chart pat (right glove)

Rnd 1 Work the 4 sets of 14 sts across.

Cont to foll chart in this way through rnd 55. The cuff and hand through the thumb gusset have been completed.

Rnd 56 Work to the 14 thumb sts (the newly made sts by M1 at the center of the chart and end of the 2nd needle, beg of the 3rd needle), sl these 14 sts to a long strand of yarn, work to end of rnd. Rejoin the sts to cont working hand and foll chart through rnd 64.

Divide for fingers

Sl the 48 sts onto 2 needles, with the first 24 sts for the back of the hand and the last 24 sts for the palm of the hand. Then, work each finger separately as foll:

Little finger

Rejoin yarn to top of hand to work sts 3–8 of chart, M1, work sts 63–68—13 sts. Divide sts evenly onto 3 dpns and k 15 rnds.

Next rnd SKP, k5, SKP, k4—11 sts. K 2 rnds.

Next rnd SKP, k4, SKP, k3—9 sts. Cut yarn and pull through all sts and draw up tightly, pull end to WS.

Ring finger

Rejoin yarn to top of the hand to work sts 9–14 of chart, M1, work sts 57–62, pick up and k 3 sts at base of little finger—16 sts. Divide sts evenly onto 3 dpns.

Next rnd K13, SK2P—14 sts. K 19 rnds.

Next rnd [SKP, k5] twice—12 sts. K 2 rnds.

Next rnd [SKP, k4] twice—10 sts. Cut yarn and pull through all sts and draw up tightly, pull end to WS.

Middle finger

Rejoin yarn to top of hand to work sts 16–21, M1, work sts 50–55, pick up and k 3 sts at base of ring finger—16 sts. Work as for ring finger only, k 23 rnds instead of 19 rnds.

Index finger

Rejoin yarn to top of hand to work sts 23–28, then sts 43–48, pick up and k 3 sts at base of middle finger—15 sts. Divide sts evenly onto 3 dpns.

Next rnd K12, SK2P—13 sts. K 18 rnds.

Next rnd SKP, k4, SKP, k5—11 sts. K 2 rnds.

Next rnd SKP, k3, SKP, k4—9 sts. Finish as for previous fingers.

Thumb

Rejoin yarn (at the back of the hand) to the 14 thumb sts on hold and divide sts evenly onto 3 dpns.

Rnd 1 K14, pick up and k 2 sts at base of thumb—16 sts.

Rnd 2 K13, k2tog, k1.

Rnd 3 SKP, K13—14 sts. K 9 rnds.

Next rnd Dec 2 sts evenly spaced around—12 sts. K 1 rnd.

Next rnd Dec 2 sts evenly spaced around—10 sts. Finish as for previous fingers.

LEFT GLOVE

Work the cuff strip as for right glove, only work the buttonhole on the 3rd and 4th rows to reverse. Foll the chart for the left glove and work the thumb and fingers as for the right glove, reversing shaping and rejoining the yarn at the palm side to beg each finger. Sew on buttons at each cuff. ✣

Wristy

These fingerless and fancy-free designs keep your digits unfettered for pedaling around town, strumming a guitar or, of course, knitting!

Business

KNITTED MEASUREMENTS

Circumference 6½"/16.5cm

Length 6½"/16.5cm

SIZE

Sized for adult woman.

MATERIALS

1 4oz/113g skein (approx 225yd/206m) of Fiesta Yarns *Swoon* (merino wool/silk) in iris (4)

Set of 5 size 8 (5mm) double-pointed needles (dpns) OR SIZE TO OBTAIN GAUGE

Stitch markers and holder

GAUGE

19 sts and 23 rnds = 4"/10cm over St st using size 8 (5mm) needles.

TAKE TIME TO CHECK GAUGE.

WRISTLETS (make 2)

Cast on 32 sts, divided evenly over 4 dpns. Place marker (pm) and join, taking care not to twist sts.

Cuff

Rnds 1–12 *K2, p2; rep from * around.

Rnds 13 and 14 Knit.

Thumb gusset

Rnd 15 K3, pm, k2, pm, k to end of rnd.

Quick and Easy Wristlets

These nifty little numbers by Kathy North are the speedy solution to cold hands. Knit in basic stockinette stitch with a ribbed border, they get their character from the variegated yarn.

Rnd 16 (inc rnd) K3, sl marker, M1, k to next marker, M1, sl marker, k to end of rnd—34 sts.

Rnd 17 Knit.

Rep last 2 rnds 5 times more—44 sts.

Next rnd (thumb opening) K3, remove marker, place next 14 sts on holder, remove marker, cast on 2 sts, k to end—32 sts.

Work even in St st until piece measures 6"/15cm from beg.

Work in k2, p2 rib for 1"/2.5cm.

Bind off loosely in rib.

Thumb

Place 14 sts from holder on dpns to work in rnds and reattach yarn.

Rnd 1 Pick up and k 4 sts along cast-on edge, k 14—18 sts.

Rnd 2 (dec rnd) [K2tog] twice, k14—16 sts.

Rnd 3 Knit.

Work in k2, p2 rib for 3 rnds. Bind off in rib. ✣

KNITTED MEASUREMENTS

Hand circumference 7"/18cm

Length (bottom of cuff to top of middle finger) 7½"/19cm

SIZE

Sized for Women's Small.

MATERIALS

1 1¾oz/50g hank (approx 125yd/114m) each of Alchemy Yarns of Transformation *Sanctuary* (wool/silk) in #42m silver (A), #21e green plum (B), #23e good earth (C), #48a passion flower (D), #92w moonstone (E), #37e twig (F), #6f poppy (G) and #82w janboy's sapphire (H) (2)

Set of 5 size 3 (3.25mm) double-pointed needles (dpns) OR SIZE TO OBTAIN GAUGE

Four ½"/13mm shank buttons

Stitch marker and holders

Scrap yarn

GAUGE

28 sts and 36 rows = 4"/10cm over St st using size 3 (3.25mm) needles.

TAKE TIME TO CHECK GAUGE.

STITCH GLOSSARY

M1R Insert LH needle from back to front under strand between last st worked and next st on LH needle, k through front loop to twist st.

M1L Insert LH needle from front to back under strand between last st worked and next st on LH needle, k through back loop to twist st.

Rainy Day Fingerless Gloves

Colorwork and duplicate stitching team up to craft a charming landscape—but these mitts do anything but fade into the background. Elli Stubenrauch's pattern begins with a flat button placket then is worked up in the round.

SEED ST (over an odd number of sts)

Row 1 *K1, p1; rep from *, end k1.

Rep row 1 for seed st.

CORRUGATED RIB (over an even number of sts)

Rnd 1 *K1 B, bring C to front of work and p1, bring C to back of work; rep from * around.

Rep rnd 1 for corrugated rib.

RIGHT GLOVE

Cuff

With A, cast on 45 sts. Working back and forth on 2 dpns, work in seed st for 4 rows.

Next (buttonhole) row (RS) K1, p1, k1, yo, k2tog, work to end.

Next row (WS) Work 5 sts in seed st, p to last 5 sts, work 5 sts in seed st.

Next row (RS) Work 5 sts in seed st, k to last 5 sts, work 5 sts in seed st.

Rep last 2 rows once more, then work 1 more WS row.

Next (buttonhole) row (RS) K1, p1, k1, yo, k2tog, work in pat as established to end.

Work 3 rows even.

Wrist

Divide sts onto 4 dpns as foll: *Needle #1* 5 sts; *Needle #2* 17 sts; *Needle #3* 18 sts; *Needle #4* 5 sts. Form a circle as for knitting in the rnd, but overlap the 5 sts on needle #4 with the 5 sts on needle #1.

Making sure the knit side is on the outside and the buttonholes are on the top, place marker (pm) and join as foll: [k 1 st on front needle tog with 1 st on back needle, p next st on front needle tog with next st on back needle] twice, k next st on front needle tog with next st on back needle, k to end of rnd—40 sts. Distribute sts evenly on 4 dpns.

Next rnd Work 5 sts in seed st, k to end of rnd.

Cont to work all sts in St st as foll:

K 2 rnds.

Work 2 rnds of chart 1. Cut A.

Next rnd With B, knit.

Next rnd *K1 B, k1 C; rep from * around.

Work in corrugated rib for 7 rnds.

Next rnd With B, knit.

Next (inc) rnd With B, *k5, M1R; rep from * around—48 sts.

Beg chart 2

Work chart rnds 1–19—64 sts.

Rnd 20 Work 24 sts, sl next 16 sts to scrap yarn for thumb, work to end of rnd—48 sts. Work through chart rnd 23.

With A, k 5 rnds.

Little finger

With A, k6, sl next 18 sts to a holder, sl next 18 sts to a 2nd holder, k last 6 sts—12 sts. K 5 rnds. Bind off purlwise.

Ring finger

Sl next 6 sts from first holder and corresponding 6 sts from 2nd holder onto working needles. Join A, leaving a long tail.

Next rnd [K6, M1R] twice—14 sts. K 5 rnds. Bind off purlwise.

Middle finger

Work as for ring finger, except k 6 rnds, instead of 5.

Index finger

Sl rem 12 sts from holders onto working needles.

Next rnd M1R, k12, M1R—14 sts. K 5 rnds. Bind off purlwise.

Thumb

Place 16 sts on scrap yarn onto working needles, join E and k 2 rnds.

Next rnd [K2 with E, k2 with A] 4 times.

With A, k 2 rnds. Bind off purlwise.

LEFT GLOVE

Work as for right glove, except work buttonholes over the last 5 seed sts as foll: K2tog, yo, k1, p1, k1. Cont as for right glove until button placket is joined. Move rnd marker to after the 5 sts of button placket and cont as for right glove.

FINISHING

Weave in all ends, using the tails to close any gaps. Embroider raindrops and apples as noted in chart 2. Block to measurements. Sew on buttons. ✣

CHART 1

CHART 2

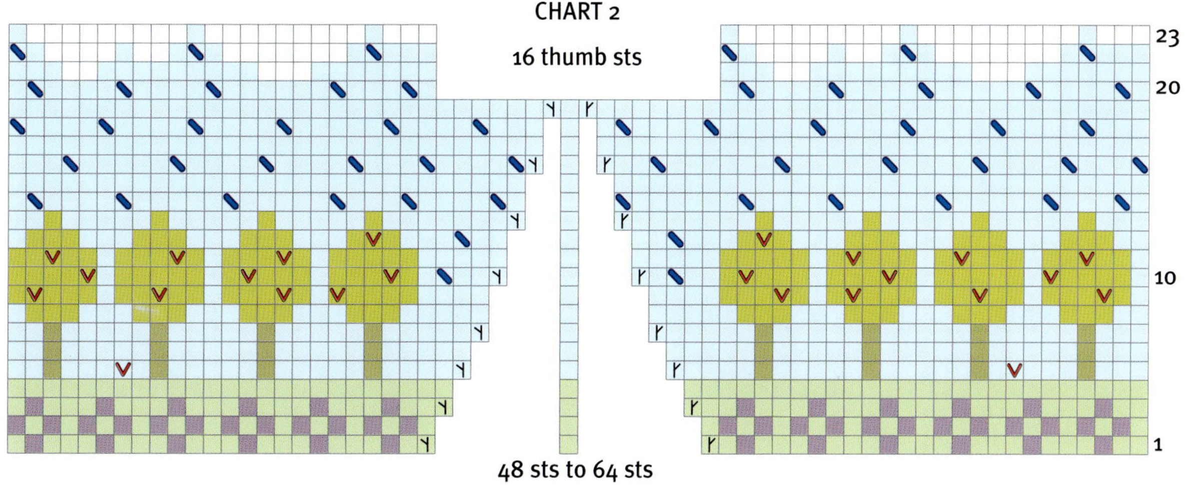

COLOR KEY

- Silver (A)
- Green Plum (B)
- Good Earth (C)
- Passion Flower (D)
- Moonstone (E)
- Twig (F)

STITCH KEY

- M1R
- M1L

EMBROIDERY KEY

- Duplicate stitch, Poppy (G)
- Left-half duplicate stitch, Janboy's Sapphire (H)

Drink Me

Lace Medallion Fingerless Gloves

These long, fingerless gloves by Mari Muinonen are formed by joining lovely lace medallions into a tube.

KNITTED MEASUREMENTS

Hand circumference 7"/18cm

Arm circumference 10"/25.5cm

Length 19"/48cm

SIZE

Sized for adult woman.

MATERIALS

2 2.6oz/74g hanks (each approx 200yd/183m) of Lorna's Laces *Shepherd Sport* (superwash wool) in denim (2)

Set of 5 size 4 (3.5mm) double-pointed needles (dpns) OR SIZE TO OBTAIN GAUGE

Stitch markers

Tapestry needle

GAUGE

24 sts and 34 rows = 4"/10cm over St st using size 4 (3.5mm) needles.

TAKE TIME TO CHECK GAUGE.

NOTE

Each glove is made using one small and one large lace medallion star. Medallions are worked in the round following the charts, with each chart rnd repeated 5 times around. Place markers between each pat rep.

SMALL STAR (make 2)

Cast on 5 sts (counts as rnd 1 of chart 1), divided over 4 needles. Place marker (pm) and join, being careful not to twist.

Cont chart 1

Chart rnd 2 [K1, yo] 5 times—10 sts.

Chart rnd 3 [K1, (k1, yo, k1) in same st] 5 times—20 sts.

Cont in chart pat through rnd 21—190 sts. Bind off loosely.

LARGE STAR (make 2)

Cast on 5 sts (counts as rnd 1 of chart 2). Pm and join, being careful not to twist.

Cont chart 2

Work chart rnds 2–25 of chart 2—190 sts. Bind off loosely.

FINISHING

Wet medallions thoroughly and pin out to block. With tapestry needle and yarn, sew points of large star to points of small star as indicated by "D" on diagram. Fold this piece in half and sew indicated points tog to form gloves. Fold top corners over to form thumb and fingers and sew in place. ✣

ASSEMBLY DIAGRAM

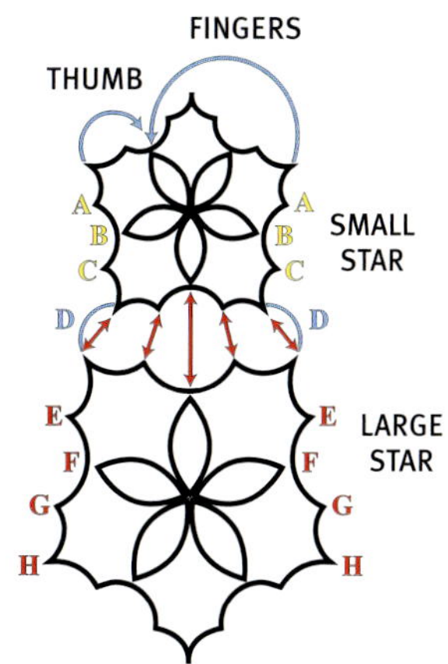

CHART 1

38 sts

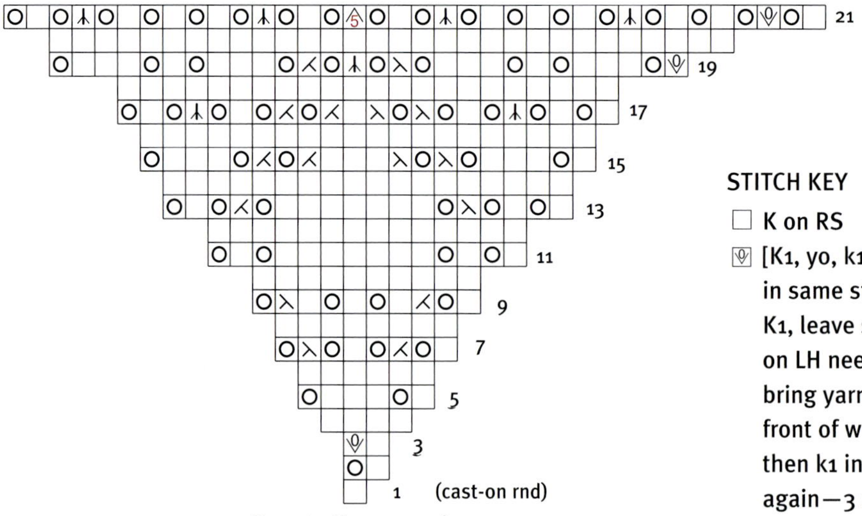
21
19
17
15
13
11
9
7
5
3
1 (cast-on rnd)

Repeat 5 times around

STITCH KEY

- K on RS
- [K1, yo, k1] in same st: K1, leave st on LH needle, bring yarn to front of work, then k1 in st again—3 sts. Sl st from LH needle.
- K2tog
- Ssk
- S2KP
- K5tog

CHART 2

38 sts

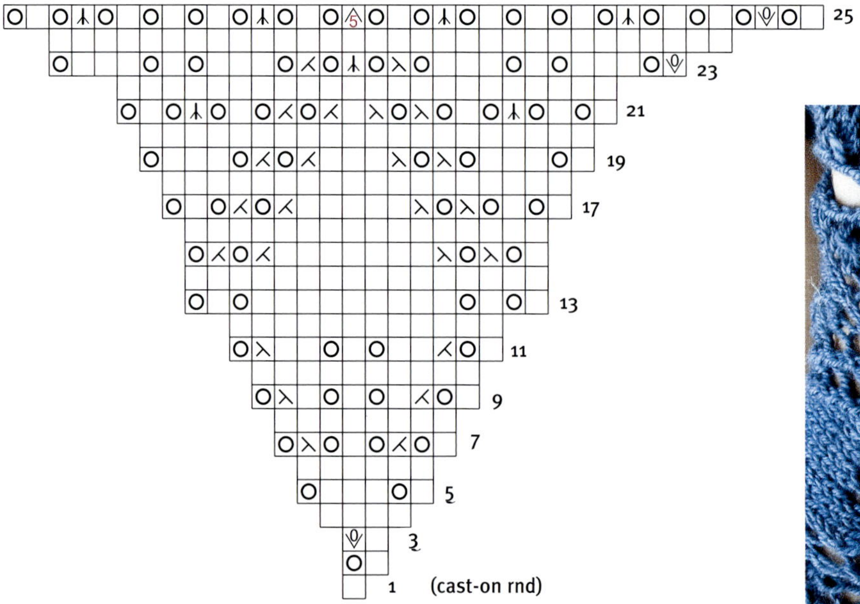
25
23
21
19
17
13
11
9
7
5
3
1 (cast-on rnd)

Repeat 5 times around

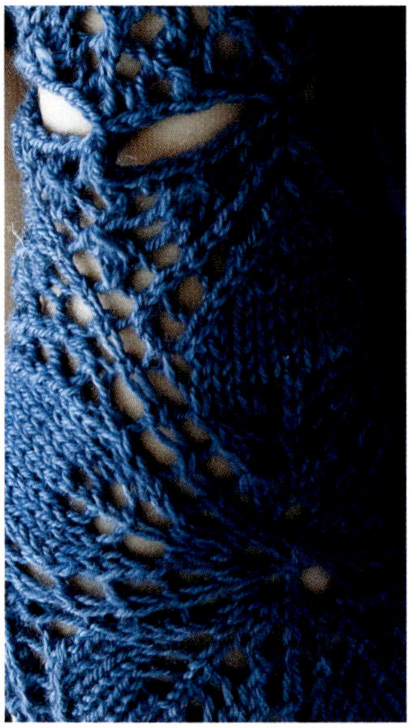

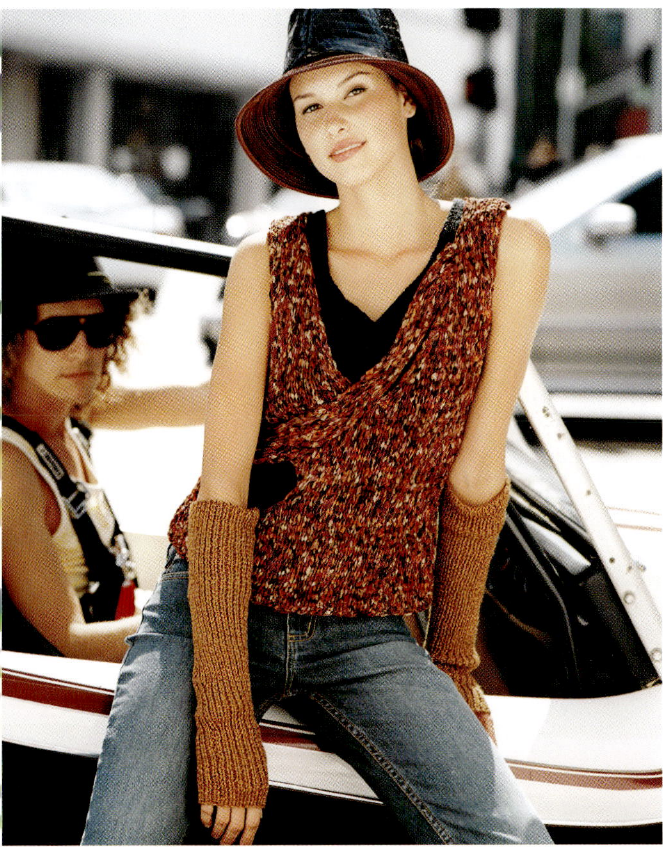

Ribbed Wristers

Knit in a softly shimmering metallic yarn, these sleek elbow-length gloves go from day to night in style.

KNITTED MEASUREMENTS

Circumference 6¾"/17cm

Length 16½"/42cm

SIZE

Sized for adult woman.

MATERIALS

3 1¾oz/50g balls (each approx 115yd/105m) of Lion Brand Yarn *Glitterspun* (acrylic/cupro/polyester) in #135 bronze (4)

One pair size 5 (3.75mm) needles OR SIZE TO OBTAIN GAUGE

GAUGE

24 sts and 32 rows = 4"/10cm over k1, p1 rib (slightly stretched) using size 5 (3.75mm) needles. TAKE TIME TO CHECK GAUGE.

GLOVES (make 2)

With size 5 (3.75mm) needles, cast on 41 sts. Work in k1, p1 rib for 1½"/4cm, end with a WS row.

Thumb opening

Next row (RS) Work 20 sts, join a 2nd ball of yarn and dec 1 st, work to end—20 sts each side. Work both sides at once with separate balls of yarn for 1"/2.5cm, end with a WS row.

Next row (RS) Work 20 sts, then using same yarn, inc 1 st in next st, work to end—41 sts. Break 2nd ball of yarn. Cont in rib, inc 1 st each side every 10th row 10 times—61 sts.

Work even until piece measures 16½"/42cm from beg. Bind off in rib. Sew back seam. ✥

Picot-Edge Gauntlets

Bring the drama with Linda Cyr's simple but sassy fingerless gauntlets. Picot-edge detailing completes the look.

KNITTED MEASUREMENTS

Hand circumference 7¼"/18.5cm

Length 7½"/19cm

SIZE

Sized for adult woman.

MATERIALS

1 2½oz/70g ball (approx 168yd/154m) of Lion Brand Yarn *Microspun* (acrylic) in #153 ebony (3)

One pair size 6 (4mm) needles OR SIZE TO OBTAIN GAUGE

Stitch markers

GAUGE

20 sts and 28 rows = 4"/10cm over St st using size 6 (4mm) needles.

TAKE TIME TO CHECK GAUGE.

GAUNTLETS (make 2)

Cast on 42 sts.

Rows 1 and 3 (RS) Knit.

Rows 2 and 4 Purl.

Row 5 (eyelet turning row) K1, *yo, k2tog; rep from *, end k1.

Rows 6 and 8 Purl.

Rows 7 and 9 Knit.

Row 10 K2, *p3, k2; rep from * to end.

Row 11 P2, *k1, yo, ssk, p2; rep from * to end.

Row 12 Rep row 10.

Row 13 P2, *k2tog, yo, k1, p2; rep from * to end.

Row 14 Rep row 10.

Rep rows 11–14 five times more.

Work in St st for 5 rows.

Thumb gusset

Next row (WS) P20, place marker (pm), p2, pm, p20.

Next row (RS) K20, sl marker, M1, k to marker, M1, sl marker, k20—44 sts.

Next row (WS) P to marker, sl marker, k to marker, sl marker, p to end. Rep last 2 rows 5 times more—54 sts (14 thumb gusset sts).

Next row (RS) K20, bind off 14 thumb gusset sts, k to end.

Next row (WS) P20, then p20 from other side of bind-off—40 sts.

Work in St st for 3 rows. K 5 rows. Bind off.

FINISHING

Turn the lower edge at the eyelet turning row to inside and seam to WS for picot edging.

Sew side seam. ✣

Slip-Stitch and Cabled Mitts

Sally Harding keeps cold hands classy in fingerless mittens with a bicolor pattern and cable-ribbed edges. They can be worn alone or over gloves when the mercury drops.

KNITTED MEASUREMENTS

Circumference around widest part of glove (slightly stretched) 7 (7½, 8)"/18 (19, 20.5)cm

SIZES

Sized for Women's Small (Medium, Large) and shown in size Small.

MATERIALS

Original Yarn

1 1¾oz/50g ball (approx 240yd/220m) each of Lane Borgosesia *Corallina* (wool) in #991 light gray (MC) and #1399 rose (CC) (1)

Substitute Yarn

1 3½oz/100g hank (approx 450yd/411m) each of Classic Elite Yarns *Alpaca Sox* (alpaca/merino wool/nylon) in #1803 ash (MC) and #1825 rose (CC) (1)

One pair size 2 (2.75mm) knitting needles OR SIZE TO OBTAIN GAUGE

Cable needle (cn)

Stitch holder

GAUGE

38 sts and 72 rows = 4"/10cm over color pat st using size 2 (2.75mm) needles.

TAKE TIME TO CHECK GAUGE.

NOTE

Mitts are worked back and forth in rows. When finishing, an invisible seam is sewn up mitt and thumb on palm side of thumb.

COLOR PAT ST (over an odd number of sts)

Row 1 (RS) With CC, *k1, sl 1 purlwise wyib; rep from *, end k1.

Row 2 With CC, purl.

Row 3 With MC, k2, *sl 1 purlwise wyib, k1; rep from *, end k1.

Row 4 With MC, purl.

Rep rows 1–4 for color pat st.

RIGHT MITT

With MC, cast on 71 sts.

Beg cable rib

Row 1 (WS) P1, *k1, p4, k1, p1 tbl; rep from *, end last rep p1, instead of p1 tbl.

Row 2 K1, *p1, sl 2 to cn and hold to *front,* k2, k2 from cn, p1, k1 tbl; rep from *, end last rep k1.

Row 3 Rep row 1.

Row 4 K1, *p1, k4, p1, k1 tbl; rep from *, end last rep k1.

Row 5 Rep row 1.

Rows 6–29 Rep rows 2–5 six times more.

Rows 30 and 31 Rep rows 4 and 5.

Rows 32–35 Rep rows 2–5.

Row 36 Rep row 2.

K 1 row, dec 8 (4, 0) sts evenly across—63 (67, 71) sts. Work in color pat st for 1¾ (2, 2)"/4.5 (5, 5)cm, end with pat row 2.

Thumb opening

Next row (RS) With MC, work color pat row 3 over first 53 (57, 59) sts, sl rem 10 (10, 12) sts onto a holder.

Next row With MC, purl.

Next row With CC, work pat row 1, then with a separate length of MC, cast on 10 (10, 12) sts onto LH needle, with CC, cont in pat across these new sts—63 (67, 71) sts. **Work even in color pat until color pat section measures 1¼ (1¼, 1½)" /3 (3, 4)cm from thumb opening, end with pat row 4. Break off CC.

Next row (RS) With MC, purl and inc 8 (4, 0) sts evenly across—71 sts. Work rows 1–10 of cable rib (thus ending with pat row 2). Bind off in pat. **

Thumb

With RS facing and CC, pick up and k 11 (11, 12) sts along cast-on edge of thumb opening, and 2 (2, 1) sts in corner, then sl 10 (10, 12) sts from holder onto needle. ***Break off CC. With RS facing, sl all 23 (23, 25) sts onto LH needle to work next row from RS. With RS facing, rejoin MC and work next row as for color pat row 3. Work even in color pat until thumb measures ¾ (¾, 1)"/2 (2, 2.5)cm, end with pat row 2. Change to MC and work 5 rows in k1, p1 rib. Bind off in rib.***

LEFT MITT

Work as for right mitt to thumb opening, end with pat row 2.

Thumb opening

Next row With RS facing, break off yarn at RH side of work, sl first 10 (10, 12) sts onto a holder, rejoin MC and work color pat row 3 over last 53 (57, 59) sts.

Next row With MC, purl to end of row, then keeping sts on holder, cast on 10 (10, 12) new sts at end of row, turn work—63 (67, 71) sts. Cont as for right mitt between ** and **.

Thumb

With RS facing, sl 10 (10, 12) sts from holder onto needle, then, with CC, pick up and k2 (2, 1) sts in corner and 11 (11, 12) sts along cast-on edge. Complete thumb as for right mitt between *** and ***.

FINISHING

Press color pat section lightly on WS with warm iron. DO NOT PRESS CABLED RIB. Sew an invisible seam along thumb and side. ✣

Supersized Wristers

Tanis Gray combines function and fashion in easy-to-knit, bulky fingerless mittens that extend above the elbow. Knit in chunky baby alpaca yarn, they are the ultimate in cozy comfort.

KNITTED MEASUREMENTS

Circumference 8"/20.5cm

Length 20"/51cm

SIZE

Sized for adult woman.

MATERIALS

2 3½oz/100g hanks (each approx 108yd/99m) of Misti Alpaca *Baby Alpaca Chunky* (baby alpaca) in #2L471 black/gray moulinette (5)

Set of 4 size 9 (5.5mm) double-pointed needles (dpns) OR SIZE TO OBTAIN GAUGE

Stitch holder

GAUGE

16 sts and 18 rnds = 4"/10cm over k1, p1 rib (slightly stretched), using size 9 (5.5mm) needles. TAKE TIME TO CHECK GAUGE.

WRISTERS (make 2)

Using size 9 dpns, cast on 32 sts. Divide evenly over 3 needles, pm for beg of rnd and join, being careful not to twist sts.

Work in k1, p1 rib until piece measures 18"/45.5cm or desired length to thumb.

Next rnd Work first 5 sts in pat as established and slip these sts to holder, cont in pat to end of rnd.

Next rnd Cast on 5 sts, cont in pat until piece measures 20"/51cm from bottom. Bind off in rib.

Thumb

Slip 5 sts from st holder to dpn. Pick up and knit 5 sts from cast-on sts over thumb opening. Divide these 10 sts on 3 dpns and work in k1, p1 rib for 1"/2.5cm.

Bind off in rib. ✣

Cabled Cozies

These long wristers by Tanis Gray, knit with a pattern of intertwining cables and hemmed with picot edges, feature a flared finish to keep your fingers free and easy.

KNITTED MEASUREMENTS

Circumference at wrist (unstretched) 6½"/16.5cm

Length 10"/25.5cm

SIZE

Sized for adult woman.

MATERIALS

3 1¾oz/50g skeins (each approx 110yd/100m) of Alpaca With A Twist *Baby Twist* (baby alpaca) in #100 natural (3)

Set of 4 size 3 (3.25mm) double-pointed needles (dpns) OR SIZE TO OBTAIN GAUGE

Size D/3 (3.25mm) crochet hook

Cable needle (cn)

Tapestry needle

Small stitch holder

Scrap yarn

GAUGES

23 sts and 30 rnds = 4"/10cm over St st using size 3 (3.25mm) needles.

35 sts and 30 rnds = 4"/10cm over chart pattern using size 3 (3.25mm) needles.

TAKE TIME TO CHECK GAUGES.

PROVISIONAL CAST-ON

Using scrap yarn and crochet hook, ch the number of cast-on sts, plus a few extra (see page 142). Cut yarn and pull the tail through the last chain to secure. With knitting needle and working yarn, pick up the required number of cast-on sts through the "purl bumps" on the back of the chain. Be careful not to split the waste yarn, as this makes it difficult to pull out the chain at the end.

When it's time to remove the chain, pull out the tail from the last ch st. Gently and slowly pull on the tail to unravel the crochet stitches, carefully placing each released knit st on a needle as you go.

STITCH GLOSSARY

8-st RPC

Sl 4 to cn, hold to *back*, k1, p2, k1; k1, p2, k1 from cn.

8-st LPC

Sl 4 to cn, hold to *front*, k1, p2, k1; k1, p2, k1 from cn.

ARM COZIES (make 2)

Cast on 44 sts, using provisional cast-on. Divide sts over 3 dpns. Place marker (pm) and join, taking care not to twist sts.

Picot edging

Rnds 1–8 Knit.

Rnd 9 (eyelet rnd) *Yo, k2tog; rep from * around.

Rnds 10–17 Knit.

Join hem

Fold hem to WS at eyelet rnd and join sts as foll (removing chain as you go): *Insert RH needle into 1 st on needle and 1 cast-on st and k these 2 sts tog; rep from * around.

Next (inc) rnd *K2, yo; rep from * around—66 sts. Divide sts evenly over 3 dpns.

Beg chart

Work 22-st rep of chart 3 times. Cont in chart

pat as established through rnd 48—60 sts.

Then rep chart rnds 25–41 once more as foll:

Work chart rnds 25 and 26.

Thumb placement

Rnd 27 K1, [p2, k2] 3 times, then sl last 10 sts just worked to a holder, cont working rnd 27 to end of rnd.

Rnd 28 K1, p2, cast on 10 sts, work in pat to end of rnd. Cont to work through chart rnd 41.

Picot edging

Work rnds 1–17 of edging as before. Fold edging in half to WS and sew live sts to first rnd of edging on WS. Cut yarn.

Thumb

K 10 sts from holder, then pick up and k 14 sts around thumb opening—24 sts. Distribute sts evenly over 3 needles. Work picot edging as for top of hand. ✥

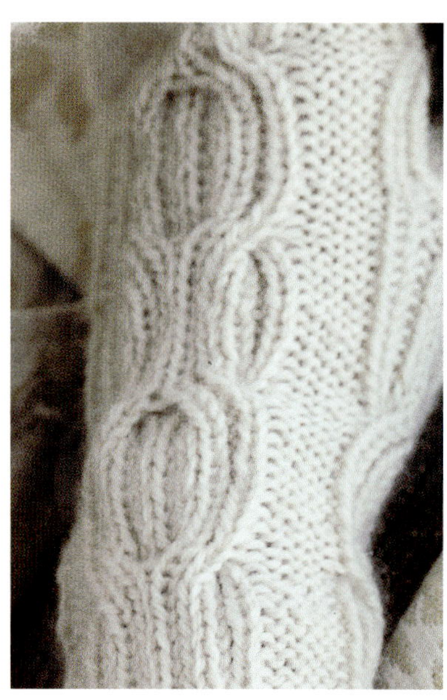

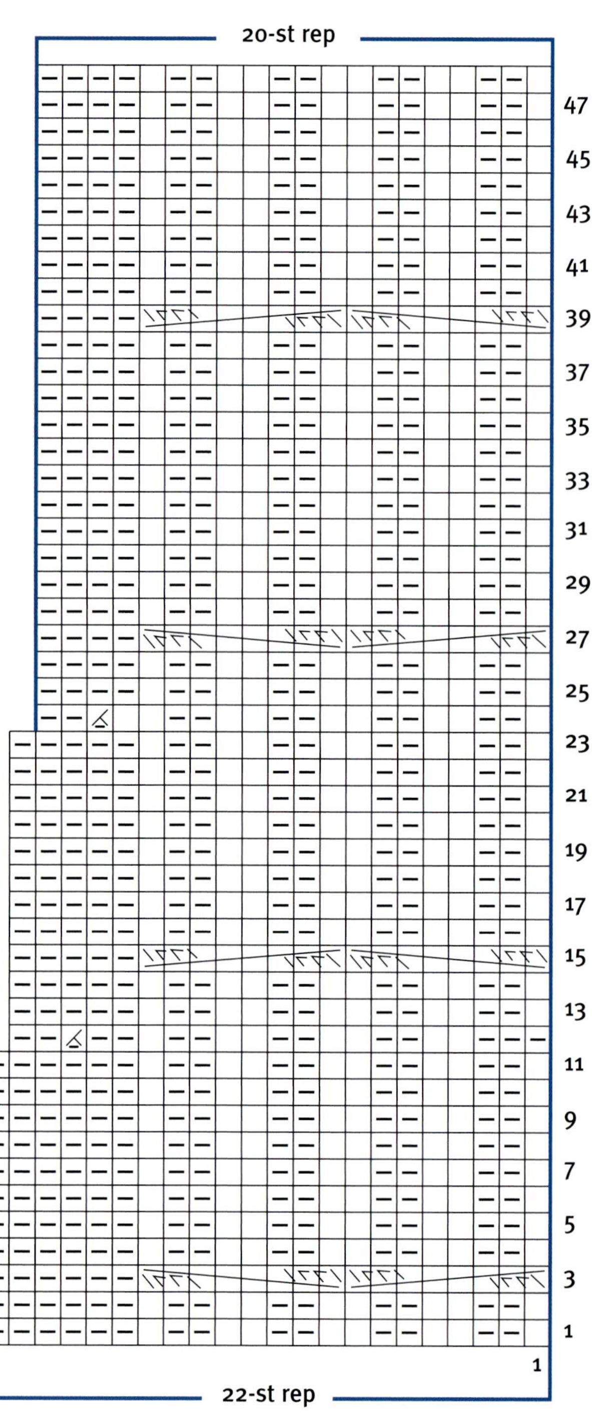

STITCH KEY

- Knit
- Purl
- P2tog
- 8-st RPC
- 8-st LPC

Ruffled Wristlets

Don a bit of Victorian flair with Tanis Gray's wristlets, featuring soft mohair-blend hands and dramatic ruffled cuffs. With minimal shaping to do, you'll be wearing them to high tea in no time.

KNITTED MEASUREMENTS

Circumference 6¾"/17cm

Length 8"/20.5cm

SIZE

Sized for adult woman.

MATERIALS

2 1¾oz/50g balls (each approx 82yd/75m) of Lion Brand *Moonlight Mohair* (acrylic/mohair/cotton/metallic polyester) in #208 arctic circle (A) (5)

2 1¾oz/50g balls (each approx 21yd/19m) of Lion Brand *Ruffles* (wool/acrylic) in #153 black (B) (6)

Set of 4 each sizes 9 and 10½ (5.5 and 6.5mm) double-pointed needles (dpns) OR SIZE TO OBTAIN GAUGE

Stitch holder and marker

GAUGE

14 sts and 18 rows = 4"/10cm using 2 strands of A held tog and larger needles.

TAKE TIME TO CHECK GAUGE.

WRISTLETS

With smaller dpns and A, cast on 24 sts, divided evenly over 3 dpns. Place marker and join.

K 2 rnds.

Change to B. P every rnd for 3"/7.5cm. Change to larger dpns and 2 strands A. K every rnd for 3"/7.5cm.

Thumbhole

Next rnd K5, place these sts on a holder, k to end of rnd.

Next rnd Cast on 5 sts, k to end of rnd. K every rnd for 2"/5cm. Bind off.

Thumb

K 5 sts from st holder, then pick up and k 7 more sts along cast-on edge—12 sts, divided evenly on 3 dpns. K every rnd for 1"/2.5cm. Bind off. ✣

Eyelet Wristers

Rock out in fingerless gloves by Robin Melanson, knitted in a twisted-column lace that will keep your wrists warm and your look cool. These wristers are finished with hand-sewn beads and sequins for an extra dose of glam.

KNITTED MEASUREMENTS

Hand circumference 7¼ (8)"/18.5 (20.5)cm

Forearm circumference 8 (8¾)"/20.5 (22)cm

Length approx 13½"/34.5cm

SIZE

Sized for Women's Small/Medium (Large/X-Large) and shown in size Small/Medium.

MATERIALS

2 1¾oz/50g hanks (each approx 110yd/100m) of Alchemy Yarns of Transformation *Synchronicity* (silk/merino wool) in blackest black (4)

One pair each sizes 6 and 10 (4 and 6mm) needles OR SIZE TO OBTAIN GAUGE

Cable needle (cn)

22 (24) each 5/16"/8mm flat sequins and seed beads to match yarn color

Stitch markers

Sewing needle and thread

GAUGE

28 sts and 22 rows = 4"/10cm over twisted column pattern.

TAKE TIME TO CHECK GAUGE.

TWISTED COLUMN PATTERN (over a multiple of 6 sts plus 4)

Set-up row (WS) With smaller needles, knit.

Row 1 (RS) With larger needles, k2. *K1, wrapping yarn twice around needle (instead of once); rep from * to last 2 sts, k2.

Row 2 With smaller needles, p2. *Sl 3 sts to RH needle, dropping all wraps, sl next 3 sts to cn, dropping all wraps, and hold to *back* of work, sl 3 sts from RH needle back to LH needle, bring cn to *front,* sl same 3 sts from LH needle back to RH needle, sl 3 sts from cn to LH needle, sl the 3 sts from RH needle to LH needle (the 2 groups of 3 sts are twisted around each other twice), p the 6 sts in their new orientation; rep from * to last 2 sts, p2.

Row 3 Knit.

Row 4 Purl.

Rep rows 1–4 for twisted column pattern.

NOTE

Be sure to change needle sizes as indicated when working in twisted column pattern.

WRISTERS (make 2)

With smaller needles, cast on 58 (64) sts. Work twisted column pat for 15 rows (ending with pat row 2).

Forearm shaping

Next (dec) row (RS—pat row 3) K26, place marker (pm), ssk, k2, k2tog, pm, k26 (32)—56 (62) sts.

Work 2 more rows in pat as established.

Next row (WS—pat row 2) Work in pat to first marker, sl next 2 sts to RH needle, dropping wraps, sl next 2 sts from LH needle to cn, dropping wraps, and hold to *back* of work, sl 2 sts from RH needle to LH needle, bring cn to *front*, sl same 2 sts from LH needle back to RH needle, sl 2 sts from cn to LH needle, sl the 2 sts from RH needle to LH needle, p the 4 sts in their new orientation, work in pat to end.

Next row Work in pat to first marker, ssk, k2tog, work to end—54 (60) sts. Work 1 row even.

Next row (RS) Work in pat to first marker, k2, work in pat to end.

Next row Work in pat to first marker, p2, work in pat to end.

Next row K to 1 st before first marker, ssk, k2tog (dropping markers), k to end—52 (58) sts.

Work 1 row even.

Work pat rows 1–4 eleven times, then rep rows 1–2 once more. P 2 rows.

Next row (RS) K2, *ssk, k2, k2tog; rep from *, end k2—36 (40) sts.

P 1 row. Bind off all sts purlwise.

FINISHING

Block wristers. Sew side seams up 10¼"/26cm from cast-on edge, and down 1½"/4cm from bound-off edge, leaving 1¾"/4.5cm open for thumb. With sewing needle and thread, sew on sequins about ½"/1.5cm apart, around edges of wristers between purl row and bind-off, with a bead in the center of each sequin. ✥

Wide-Rib Fingerless Gloves

Ribbed arm warmers have never been more stunning than in Judy Sumner's button-detail design knit in shimmering yarn. They'll put you at peace with "baring" arms.

KNITTED MEASUREMENTS

Width at top (unstretched) 6¾"/17cm

Length 18½"/47cm

SIZE

Sized for adult woman.

MATERIALS

3 1¾oz/50g skeins (each approx 115yd/105m) of Lion Brand Yarn *Glitterspun* (acrylic/polyester/cupro) in #135 bronze (4)

Set of 4 each sizes 6 and 8 (4 and 5mm) double-pointed needles (dpns)

Fourteen ⅝"/15mm buttons

Stitch marker

GAUGE

24 sts and 30 rows = 4"/10cm over k2, p2 rib (unstretched) using larger needles.

TAKE TIME TO CHECK GAUGE.

FINGERLESS GLOVES (make 2)

With larger dpn, cast on 40 sts, divided over 3 dpns. Place marker and join. Work in k2, p2 rib for 10"/25.5cm. Change to smaller dpns. Cont in rib pat until piece measures 18"/45.5cm from beg.

Thumbhole

Next rnd Bind off 8 sts, work to end.

Next rnd Work in rib pat, joining to next st on needle past thumbhole. Rib 2 more rnds. Bind off.

FINISHING

Sew 7 buttons in the center top of each glove, the first one approx 3½"/9cm from the bound-off edge and the other six spaced ½"/1.5cm apart. ✣

Seed-Stitch Mitts and Scarf Combo

Keep your fingers free with these simple wrist warmers and complementary scarf by Debbie Bliss, knit in two subtly different shades of blue to keep things interesting. The super-soft mitts are knit in the round.

KNITTED MEASUREMENTS

Scarf Width 6¼"/16cm; Length 35"/89cm

Wrist warmers Circumference 8"/20.5cm

Length 11"/28cm

SIZE

Sized for adult woman.

MATERIALS

Scarf 2 3½oz/100g balls (each approx 86yd/79m) of Debbie Bliss/KFI *Cashmerino Super Chunky* (wool/microfiber/cashmere) in #23 duck egg (A) (5)

One pair size 11 (8mm) needles OR SIZE TO OBTAIN GAUGE

Wrist warmers

Original Yarn

3 1¾oz/50g balls (each approx 66yd/61m) of Debbie Bliss/KFI *Baby Alpaca Silk* (alpaca/silk) in #17 duck egg (B) (4)

Substitute Yarn

3 1¾oz/50g balls (each approx 66yd/60m) of Debbie Bliss/KFI *Alpaca Silk Aran* (alpaca/silk) in #37 sky (4)

Set of 4 each sizes 6 and 7 (4 and 4.5mm) double-pointed needles (dpns) OR SIZE TO OBTAIN GAUGE

GAUGES

Scarf 13 sts and 22 rows = 4"/10cm over seed st using size 11 (8mm) needles and A.

Wrist warmers 18 sts and 32 rows = 4"/10cm over seed st using size 7 (4.5mm) needles and B.

TAKE TIME TO CHECK GAUGES.

SEED STITCH (worked back and forth over an odd number of sts)

Row 1 K1, *p1, k1; rep from * to end.

Rep row 1 for seed st.

SEED STITCH (worked circularly over an even number of sts)

Rnd 1 *K1, p1; rep from * around.

Rnd 2 *P1, k1; rep from * around.

Rep rnds 1 and 2 for seed st.

SCARF

With size 11 (8mm) needles and A, cast on 21 sts.

Work seed st (back and forth) until piece measures 10"/25.5cm from beg.

Loop joining

Next row Bring cast-on edge up behind sts on needle, then work in pat, at same time working each st on needle tog with a corresponding st on cast-on edge.

Work even until piece measures 30"/76cm from loop joining. Bind off.

MITTS (make 2)

With size 7 (4.5mm) dpn and B, cast on 36 sts, divided over 3 dpns. Pm and join.

Work seed st (circularly) until piece measures 6¾"/17cm from beg. Change to size 6 (4mm) dpns and cont in pat until piece measures 9½"/23cm from beg.

Thumb opening

Next rnd Work in pat over 15 sts, bind off next 6 sts, work in pat to end—30 sts.

Next rnd Work in pat over 15 sts, cast on 2 sts, work in pat to end—32 sts. Work even until piece measures 11"/28cm from beg. Bind off in pat. ✣

Fun &

Playful muffs, handy flip mittens, luscious arm warmers and more run the gamut from pretty practicality to frivolous fun.

Funky

Sporty Chevron Arm Warmers

Go nuts for neon in these zig-zag striped arm warmers—or get kicky by wearing them on your legs! Linda Cyr's pattern is worked in chevron-pattern rows and seamed to finish.

KNITTED MEASUREMENTS

Circumference at wrist (ankle) 9 (10¾)"/23 (27)cm

Circumference at arm (leg) 12½ (14)"/31.5 (35.5)cm

Length 16½ (18)"/42 (45.5)cm

SIZE

Sized for adult woman.

MATERIALS

Original Yarns

1 1¾oz/50g ball (approx 116yd/104m) each of Dale of Norway *Neon Falk* (wool) in #144 pink (A), #184 green (B), #130 orange (C), #138 red (D) and #120 yellow (E) (3)

Substitute Yarns

1 1¾oz/50g ball (approx 116yd/106m) each of Dale of Norway *Falk* (superwash wool) in #4516 pink (A), #8817 green (B), #3309 orange (C), #4018 red (D) and #2427 yellow (E) (3)

One pair size 6 (4mm) needles OR SIZE TO OBTAIN GAUGE

GAUGE

28 sts and 27 rows = 4"/10cm over pat st using size 6 (4mm) needles.

TAKE TIME TO CHECK GAUGE.

STITCH GLOSSARY

Double Dec

Sl 2 tog knitwise, k1, pass 2 slipped sts over k1—2 sts dec'd.

Double Inc

[K1, yo, k1] in same st—2 sts inc'd.

PATTERN STITCH

(beg with a multiple of 12 sts plus 15)

Row 1 K1, ssk, *k9, double dec; rep from *, end k9, k2tog, k1.

Row 2 P2, *k4, double inc, k4, p1; rep from * end p1.

Rep rows 1 and 2 for pat st.

STRIPE PATTERN (40-ROW REP)

Work 2 rows each with *A, B, C, D, A, E, B, D, C, E, A, D, B, C, A, E, D, C, B, E; rep from * for stripe pat.

NOTE

Instructions are for arm warmers. Changes for leg warmers are in parentheses. If there is only one number, it applies to both styles.

WARMERS (make 2)

With A, cast on 63 (75) sts. Work in pat st and stripe pat for 60 rows. Cont in pats as foll:

Beg shaping

Row 1 K3, [k9, double dec] 4 (5) times, k9, k2tog, k1.

Row 2 P2, [k4, double inc, k4, p1] 4 (5) times, k4, double inc, k5, p2.

Row 3 K1, ssk, k11, k2tog, [k9, double dec] 3 (4) times, k9, k2tog, k1.

Row 4 P2, [k4, double inc, k4, p1] 4 (5) times, k5, double inc, k5, p2.

Row 5 K1, ssk, k11, ssk, k10, [double dec, k9] 3 (4) times, k2tog, k1.

Row 6 P2, [k4, double inc, k4, p1] 3 (4) times, k4, double inc, k5, p1, k5, double inc, k5, p2.

Row 7 K1, ssk, k11, double dec, k11, k2tog, [k9, double dec] 2 (3) times, k9, k2tog, k1.

Row 8 P2, [k4, double inc, k4, p1] 3 (4) times, [k5, double inc, k5, p1] twice, p1.

Row 9 K1, ssk, k11, double dec, k11, ssk, k10, [double dec, k9] 2 (3) times, k2tog, k1.

Row 10 P2, [k4, double inc, k4, p1] 2 (3) times, k4, [double inc, k5, p1, k5] twice, double inc, k5, p2.

Row 11 K1, ssk, [k11, double dec] twice, k11, k2tog, [k9, double dec] 1 (2) times, k9, k2tog, k1.

Row 12 P2, [k4, double inc, k4, p1] 2 (3) times, [k5, double inc, k5, p1] 3 times, p1.

Row 13 K1, ssk, [k11, double dec] twice, k11, ssk, k10, [double dec, k9] 1 (2) times, k2tog, k1.

Row 14 P2, [k4, double inc, k4, p1] 1 (2) times, k4, [double inc, k5, p1, k5] 3 times, double inc, k5, p2.

Row 15 K1, ssk, [k11, double dec] 3 times, k11, k2tog, k9, [double dec, k9] 0 (1) times, k2tog, k1.

Row 16 P2, [k4, double inc, k4, p1] 1 (2) times, [k5, double inc, k5, p1] 4 times, p1.

Row 17 K1, ssk, [k11, double dec] 3 times, k11, ssk, k10, [double dec, k9] 0 (1) time, k2tog, k1.

Row 18 P2, [k4, double inc, k4, p1] 0 (1) time, k4, [double inc, k5, p1, k5] 4 times, double inc, k5, p2.

Row 19 K1, ssk, [k11, double dec] 4 times, k11, [k2tog, k9] 0 (1) time, k2tog, k1.

Row 20 P2, [k4, double inc, k4, p1] 0 (1) time, [k5, double inc, k5, p1] 5 times, p1.

Leg warmers only

Row 21 K1, ssk, [k11, double dec] 4 times, k11, ssk, k10, k2tog, k1.

Row 22 P2, k4, [double inc, k5, p1, k5] 5 times, double inc, k5, p2.

Row 23 K1, ssk, [k11, double dec] 5 times, k13.

Row 24 P2, [k5, double inc, k5, p1] 6 times, p1.

Both styles

Rep rows 1–20 (1–24) once more, changing all k4's to k5, k5's to k6, k9's to k11, k10's to k12, and k11's to k13—83 (99) sts.

Next row (RS) K1, ssk, [k13, double dec] 4 (5) times, k13, k2tog, k1—73 (87) sts.

Next row P2, [k6, double inc, k6, p1] 5 (6) times, end p1—83 (99) sts. Rep last 2 rows 5 times more, or to desired length.

Bind off all sts.

FINISHING

Sew seam. ✣

Fold-Over Mitten-Gloves

Fingerless gloves and convertible mittens make a happy marriage in Jenn Jarvis's innovative combination. (A button anchor ensures that the flip cap doesn't flap.)

KNITTED MEASUREMENTS

Circumference 7 (7½, 8)"/18 (19, 20.5)cm

SIZE

Sized for Women's Small (Medium, Large) and shown in size Small.

MATERIALS

1 2oz/57g hank (approx 215yd/197m) each of Lorna's Laces *Shepherd Sock* (superwash wool/nylon) in #29ns pale pink (A) and #36ns chocolate (B) (1)

Set of 5 size 2 (2.75mm) double-pointed needles (dpns) OR SIZE TO OBTAIN GAUGE

Size C/2 (2.75mm) crochet hook

Two ½"/1.5cm buttons

Stitch markers and holder

GAUGE

28 sts and 40 rows = 4"/10cm over St st using size 2 (2.75mm) needles.

TAKE TIME TO CHECK GAUGE.

CORRUGATED RIB (over a multiple of 4 sts)

Rnd 1 *Bring B to front of work, p2, bring B to back of work, with A, k2; rep from * to end.

Rep rnd 1 for corrugated rib.

RIGHT MITTEN

Cuff

With B, cast on 48 (52, 56) sts, divided evenly over 4 dpns. Place marker (pm) and join. Work in corrugated rib until piece measures 2½ (2¾, 2¾)"/6.5 (7, 7)cm. Cut B.

Change to A and St st.

Next rnd Knit, inc 1 st—49 (53, 57) sts.

Thumb gusset

Inc rnd 1 K26 (28, 30), pm, M1, k1, M1, pm, k to end of rnd—51 (55, 59) sts.

Next 2 rnds Knit.

Inc rnd 2 K to first marker, sl marker, M1, k to 2nd marker, M1, sl marker, k to end—53 (57, 61) sts.

Rep inc rnd 2 every 3rd rnd 5 (6, 7) times more—63 (69, 75) sts, and 15 (17, 19) sts between markers.

Next rnd K to first marker, place 15 (17, 19) sts between markers on a holder (removing markers), cast on 1 st, k to end of rnd—49 (53, 57) sts. Work in St st until piece measures 6 (6½, 6¾)"/15 (16.5, 17)cm from beg.

Little finger

K6 (6, 7), place 38 (42, 44) sts on holder, cast on 1 st, k5 (5, 6)—12 (12, 14) sts. K 4 rnds. Cut A, attach B. K 1 rnd. Bind off.

Upper hand

Return 38 (42, 44) sts to needles. With A, pick up and k 2 sts at base of little finger, k38 (42, 44)—40 (44, 46) sts. K 3 rnds.

Ring finger

K7 (8, 8), place 26 (28, 30) sts on holder, cast on 1 (1, 2) st, k7 (8, 8)—15 (17, 18) sts. K 6 rnds. Cut A, attach B. K 1 rnd. Bind off.

Middle finger

Place first and last 6 (7, 7) held sts on needles. With A, pick up and k 2 sts at base of ring finger, k6 (7, 7), cast on 2 sts, k6 (7, 7)—16 (18, 18) sts. K 6 rnds. Cut A, attach B. K 1 rnd. Bind off.

Index finger

Place rem 14 (14, 16) sts on needles. With A, pick up and k 1 (2, 2) st at base of middle finger, k14 (14, 16)—15 (16, 18) sts. K 6 rnds. Cut A, attach B. K 1 rnd. Bind off.

Thumb

Place 15 (17, 19) gusset sts on 3 dpns, pick up and k1 st from cast-on st—16 (18, 20) sts. Work in St st until piece measures 2 (2¼, 2½)"/5 (5.5, 6.5)cm.

Next 1 (2, 2) rnds *K2tog; rep from * to end. Cut yarn, leaving a long tail. Thread through rem 8 (5, 5) sts and cinch tightly to close.

MITTEN CAP

With B, cast on 48 (52, 56) sts, divide over 4 dpns. Work in corrugated rib until piece measures 1"/2.5cm. Cut B, work in St st with A until piece measures 2½ (2¾, 3)"/6.5 (7, 7.5)cm from beg.

Next (dec) rnd *Needle #1* K1, ssk, k to end; *Needle #2* K to last 3 sts, k2tog, k1; *Needle #3* K1, ssk, k to end; *Needle #4* K to last 3 sts, k2tog, k 1—44 (48, 52) sts. Rep dec rnd every other rnd 3 times more, then every rnd 3 (3, 4) times—20 (24, 24) sts. Join sts, using 3-needle bind-off (see page 144).

LEFT MITTEN

Work as for right mitten, except work inc rnd 1 of thumb gusset as foll:

Next rnd K22 (24, 26), pm, M1, k1, M1, pm, k to end of rnd.

FINISHING

Sew mitten tops to backs of gloves below fingers.

Button loops (make 2)

With B and crochet hook, ch 7. Fasten off. Thread chain through center top of mitten cap. Sew buttons to ribbing on mittens, opposite button loops. ✣

Snowball Muff

You can be an ice queen and still keep your hands warm with Lisa Buccellato's glittery fur muff, complete with a strap to keep it in place. The muff is knitted flat and sewn into a tube during finishing.

KNITTED MEASUREMENTS

Muff Circumference 12"/30.5cm

Length 21"/54cm

Strap Length 32"/81cm

SIZE

Sized for adult woman.

MATERIALS

2 1¾oz/50g balls (each approx 115yd/105m) of Lion Brand *Glitterspun* (acrylic/polyester/cupro) in #150 silver (A) (4)

3 1¾oz/50g balls (each approx 55yd/50m) of Lion Brand *Festive Fur* (polyester/metallic polyester) in #150 silver (B) (4)

One pair size 9 (5.5mm) needles OR SIZE TO OBTAIN GAUGE

GAUGE

16 sts and 22 rows = 4"/10cm over k2, p2 rib using 2 strands of A held tog. TAKE TIME TO CHECK GAUGE.

NOTE

Keep 1 st at each edge in garter st for selvage.

MUFF

With 2 strands of A held tog, cast on 30 sts.

Row 1 Knit.

Row 2 K1, p to last st, k1. Rep last 2 rows until piece measures 1"/2.5cm from beg, end with a WS row.

Beg k2, p2 rib

Row 1 (RS) K1, *k2, p2; rep from *, end k1. Rep row 1 until rib measures 5"/12.5 cm above St st roll, end with a RS row.

Inc row (WS) K1, *p into front and back of next st, p1; rep from *, end k1—44 sts.

Break 1 strand of A.

Next row (RS) With 1 strand of A and 2 strands of B held tog, k1, p to last st, k1.

Next row Knit. Rep last 2 rows until fur portion measures 9"/23cm, end with a RS row. Break 2 strands of B.

Dec row (WS) With 2 strands of A held tog, k1, *p2tog, p1; rep from *, end k1—30 sts.

Work in k2, p2 rib for 5"/12.5cm, then work in St st for 1"/2.5cm. Bind off.

STRAP

With 2 strands of A held tog, cast on 144 sts. K 1 row. Bind off purlwise.

FINISHING

Fold muff in half lengthwise with RS tog. With 1 strand A, sew side seams. Turn muff RS out. Sew ends of strap to seam at juncture between ribbing and fur portions. ✣

Lovers' Mitten

This unique design by Jennifer Carter makes holding hands even more fun.

KNITTED MEASUREMENTS

Length 9"/23cm

Main body circumference 14"/35.5cm

Smaller cuff stretches to 10"/25.5cm

Larger cuff stretches to 12"/30.5cm

SIZE

Sized for adult man and woman.

MATERIALS

1 1½oz/40g ball (approx 84yd/71m) each of Lion Brand Yarn *Lion Cashmere Blend* (merino/cashmere/nylon) in #113 red (A), #105 light blue (B) and #098 cream (C) (4)

One pair size 8 (5mm) needles

Tapestry needle

Stitch holder

GAUGE

18 sts and 24 rows = 4"/10cm over St st using size 8 (5mm) needles.

TAKE TIME TO CHECK GAUGE.

MITTEN

Hand

With A, cast on 12 sts.

Row 1 [K into front and back of a st (kfb)] 12 times—24 sts.

Row 2 and all WS rows Purl.

Row 3 *[Kfb] 3 times, k6, [kfb] 3 times; rep from * once more—36 sts.

Row 5 *K1, [kfb] 3 times, k10, [kfb] 3 times, k1; rep from * once more—48 sts.

Row 7 *K1, [kfb] 3 times, k8, M1, k8, [kfb] 3 times, k1; rep from * once more—62 sts.

Work in St st for 9 rows.

Beg chart pat

Row 1 (RS) K1, work 6-st rep of chart 10 times, k1. Keeping 1 st each side in garter st (for selvage), cont in chart pat as established for 10 rows more. With A, work in St st until piece measures 6"/15cm from beg, end with a RS row.

Next row (WS) Purl, dec 10 sts evenly across—52 sts.

Larger cuff

Next row (RS) Cable cast on 14 sts, then k 40 sts, place rem 26 sts on a st holder, turn work. Work over these 40 sts as foll:

Work 3 rows even.

Next row (RS) Knit, dec 8 sts evenly across—32 sts.

Work in k2, p2 rib for 1½"/3.75cm, end with a WS row. With B, rib 1 row. With C, rib 1 row. Rib 2 rows with A. Bind off loosely.

Smaller cuff

Return to 26 sts on st holder.

With RS facing, join A and k 1 row.

Next row (WS) Cable cast on 14 sts, p to end—40 sts. Work 3 rows even.

Next row (WS) Purl, dec 12 sts evenly across—28 sts.

Work in k2, p2 rib for 2"/5cm.

Bind off loosely.

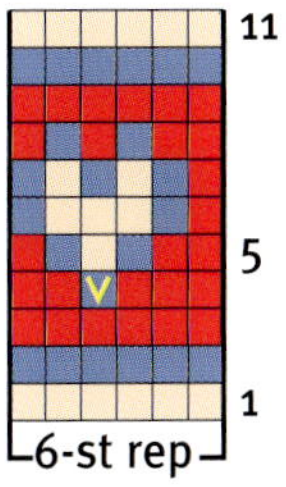

11

5

1

6-st rep

COLOR KEY

Red

Light Blue

Cream

Duplicate stitch (in Light Blue)

STITCH KEY

K on RS, p on WS

FINISHING

With B, work duplicate st on row 4 of chart pat for each pat rep, to form the base of each heart. Sew side seam from cast-on edge to the cable cast-on. Sew cable cast-on edges tog. Sew each cuff seam. ✣

Button-On Sleeves

Get up in arms for Kellie Overbey's knitted sleeves: They're as easy to knit as they are to add to your favorite old T-shirt. Buttons allow you to take them on and off as you choose.

KNITTED MEASUREMENTS

Circumference (unstretched) 8 (9¼, 10¾)"/20.5 (23.5, 27.5)cm

SIZE

Sized for Women's Small (Medium, Large) and shown in size Small.

MATERIALS

2 (3, 3) 1¾oz/50g balls (each approx 110yd/100m) of Lion Brand *Incredible* (nylon) in #208 copper penny (6)

One pair size 15 (10mm) needles OR SIZE TO OBTAIN GAUGE

T-shirt with short cap sleeves

Twelve ¾"/19mm buttons

GAUGE

12 sts and 12 rows = 4"/10cm over St st using size 15 (10mm) needles.

TAKE TIME TO CHECK GAUGE.

SLEEVES

Cast on 24 (28, 32) sts. Work in St st until piece measures 2½"/6.5cm less than total desired length from edge of T-shirt sleeve to wrist.

K 10 rows. Bind off. Sew seam.

FINISHING

Sew 6 buttons evenly spaced around edge of each T-shirt sleeve. Attach knitted sleeve to T-shirt sleeve by pulling buttons through sts at top of knitted sleeve. ✣

Crocheted Muff and Earflap Hat

This muff by Mari Tobita uses a unique crochet stitch for a herringbone-like texture. The knitted hat with crocheted earflaps makes it a charming set.

KNITTED MEASUREMENTS

Hat Head circumference 16½"/42cm (unstretched; stretches to fit most sizes)

Muff Circumference 16"/40.5cm

SIZE

Sized for adult woman.

MATERIALS

Muff

3 1¾oz/50g balls (each approx 120yd/110m) of Zitron/Skacel Collection, Inc. *Ecco* (merino wool) in #101 ecru (MC) (4)

2 .4oz/10g balls (each approx 27yd/25m) of Schulana/Skacel Collection, Inc. *Angora Schulana* (angora) in #44 aqua (A) (4)

Hat

2 balls of *Ecco* in #101 ecru (MC)

2 balls each of *Angora Schulana* in #44 aqua (A) and #15 white (B)

Size G/6 (4mm) crochet hook OR SIZE TO OBTAIN GAUGE

One size 6 (4mm) circular needle 16"/40cm long OR SIZE TO OBTAIN GAUGE

Set of 5 size 6 (4mm) double-pointed needles (dpns) OR SIZE TO OBTAIN GAUGE

Stitch marker

GAUGES

12 sts and 10 rows = 4"/10cm over puff st using size G/6 (4mm) crochet hook.

23 sts and 32 rows = 4"/10cm over St st using size 6 (4mm) needles.

32 sts and 32 rnds = 4"/10cm over k1, p1 rib (unstretched) using size 6 (4mm) needles.

TAKE TIME TO CHECK GAUGES.

PUFF STITCH

(**Note** This pattern is a one-row pattern that is reversible. The st slants left on both sides and must be worked back and forth. See page 135 for how-tos.) [Yo, insert hook, yo and draw through a loop] 6 times, yo, draw through 13 loops on hook.

Chain a multiple of 2 sts.

Foundation row Sc in 2nd ch from hook *[yo, insert hook behind ch st, yo, draw through a loop] 6 times, yo, draw through 13 loops on hook, ch 1, skip 1 ch, sc in next ch; rep from *, end dc in last ch, turn.

Row 1 Ch 1, *sc in side of next puff st (below head of st), work puff st in ch-1 before (or to the right of) same puff st, ch 1; rep from *, end dc in space below last puff st of previous row, turn.

Rep row 1 for puff st.

MUFF

(**Note** Piece is worked back and forth, even though the piece is round.)

With A, very loosely ch 50. Join with sl st to beg of ch, being careful not to twist sts.

Rnd 1 (RS) Ch 1, *skip 1 ch, sc in next ch, [yo, insert hook behind ch st, yo, draw through a loop] 6 times, yo, draw through 13 loops on hook, ch 1; rep from to end. Join with sl st to beg of ch, ch 1, turn so that WS is facing.

Rnd 2 (WS) *Sc in side, puff st behind ch-1 space, ch 1; rep from * to end. Join with sl st to beg of ch, ch 1, turn. Change to MC and rep rnd 2, alternate facing RS and WS until piece measures approx 9"/23cm. Change to A and work 2 rnds. Cut yarn and weave in ends.

HAT

With circular needle, cast on 132 sts. Place marker and join. Work in k1, p1 rib for 32 rnds.

Top shaping

(**Note** Switch to dpns when sts no longer fit on circular.)

Rnd 33 *[K1, p1] 9 times, k1, k2tog, p1; rep from * around—126 sts.

Rnd 34 *[K1, p1] 9 times, k2, p1; rep from * around.

Rnd 35 *[K1, p1] 9 times, k2tog, p1; rep from * around—120 sts.

Rnd 36 *K1, p1; rep from * around.

Rnd 37 *[K1, p1] 8 times, k1, k2tog, p1; rep from * around—114 sts.

Rnd 38 *[K1, p1] 8 times, k2, p1; rep from * around.

Rnd 39 *[K1, p1] 8 times, k2tog, p1; rep from * around—108 sts.

Rnd 40 *K1, p1; rep from * around.

Rnd 41 *[K1, p1] 7 times, k1, k2tog, p1; rep from * around—102 sts.

Rnd 42 *[K1, p1] 7 times, k2, p1; rep from * around.

Rnd 43 *[K1, p1] 7 times, k2tog, p1; rep from * around—96 sts.

Rnd 44 *K1, p1; rep from * around.

Rnd 45 *[K1, p1] 6 times, k1, k2tog, p1; rep from * around—90 sts.

Rnd 46 *[K1, p1] 6 times, k2, p1; rep from * around.

Rnd 47 *[K1, p1] 6 times, k2tog, p1; rep from * around—84 sts.

Rnd 48 *K1, p1; rep from * around.

Rnd 49 *[K1, p1] 5 times, k1, k2tog, p1; rep from * around—78 sts.

Rnd 50 *[K1, p1] 5 times, k2, p1; rep from * around.

Rnd 51 *[K1, p1] 5 times, k2tog, p1; rep from* around—72 sts.

Rnd 52 *K1, p1; rep from * around.

Rnd 53 *[K1, p1] 4 times, k1, k2tog, p1; rep from * around—66 sts.

Rnd 54 *[K1, p1] 4 times, k2, p1; rep from * around.

Rnd 55 *[K1, p1] 4 times, k2tog, p1; rep from * around—60 sts.

Rnd 56 *K1, p1; rep from * around.

Rnd 57 *[K1, p1] 3 times, k1, k2tog, p1; rep from * around—54 sts.

Rnd 58 *[K1, p1] 3 times, k2, p1; rep from * around.

Rnd 59 *[K1, p1] 3 times, k2tog, p1; rep from * around—48 sts.

Rnd 60 *K1, p1; rep from * around.

Rnd 61 *[K1, p1] twice, k1, k2tog, p1; rep from * around—42 sts.

Rnd 62 *[K1, p1] twice, k2, p1; rep from * around.

Rnd 63 *[K1, p1] twice, k2tog, p1; rep from * around—36 sts.

Rnd 64 *K1, p1; rep from * around.

Rnd 65 *K1, p1, k1, k2tog, p1; rep from * around—30 sts.

Rnd 66 *K1, p1, k2, p1; rep from * around.

Rnd 67 *K1, p1, k2tog, p1; rep from * around—24 sts.

Rnd 68 *K1, p1; rep from * around.

Rnd 69 *K1, k2tog, p1; rep from * around—18 sts.

Rnd 70 *K2, p1; rep from * around.

Rnd 71 *K2tog, p1; rep from * around—12 sts.

Rnd 72 *K1, p1; rep from * around.

Rnd 73 Sl 1, [k2tog] 5 times, k last st of rnd tog with sl st. Cut yarn and draw through rem 6 sts. Pull tightly to close. Weave in ends.

EARFLAPS AND CORDS (make 2)

With A, loop twice around finger, insert hook through loop and draw through a loop.

Rnd 1 Ch 2, *work puff st in loop, ch 2; rep from * 5

times more—6 puff sts. Change to B, join the sl st to beg of ch.

Rnd 2 Ch1, sc in head of puff st, work puff st in ch-1 before (or to the right of) same puff st, ch 1; *sc in next ch-1 space, puff st behind head of puff st, ch 1, sc in head of puff st, puff st in ch-1 before (or to the right of) same puff st, ch 1; rep from * 4 more times, sc in ch-1 space, puff st behind head of puff st, ch 1. Join the sl st to beg of ch, turn so WS is facing.

Rnd 3 Ch1, sc in ch-1 space, puff st in ch-1 before (or to the right of) same puff st, ch 1, *sc in side of puff st, puff st behind head of puff st, ch 1, sc in head of puff st, puff st in ch-1 before (or to the right of) same puff st, ch 1, sc in side of puff st, puff st behind head of puff st, ch 1; rep from * 4 times more, sc in side of puff st, puff st in ch-1 before (or to the right of) same puff st, ch 1, sc in next ch-1 space, puff st behind head of puff st, ch 1. Change to yarn A. Join the sl st to beg of ch, turn so that RS facing.

Rnd 4 Ch 1, sc in ch-1 space, puff st in ch-1 before (or to right of) same puff st, ch 1, sc in side of puff st, puff st in ch-1 before (or to right of) same puff st, ch 1, *[sc in side of puff st, puff st behind ch-1 space, ch 1] twice, sc in head, puff st behind ch-1 space, ch 1, sc in side, puff st behind head, ch 1; rep from * 4 times more, [sc in side, puff st behind ch-1 space, ch 1] twice, sc in next ch-1 space, puff st behind head of puff st, ch 1. Join the sl st to beg of ch, turn so that WS is facing. Cut yarn and weave in ends. With MC and 2 dpns, pick up 4 sts from last B row of earflap, *k4, do not turn, slide sts to beg of needle to work next row from RS; rep from * for 16"/40.5cm. Insert hook 4 sts from dpn, work sl st.

Change to A, ch 15. Insert hook to 3rd ch, [yo, insert hook, yo and draw through a loop] 6 times, insert hook to 4th ch from bottom of puff st, yo, draw through hook. Sl st, *ch 3, insert hook to 3rd ch, [yo, insert hook, yo and draw through a loop] 6 times, insert hook to 4th ch from bottom of puff st, yo, draw through hook. Rep from * one more time. Cut yarn and weave in ends.

FINISHING

Sew one ear flap to each side of hat.✣

PUFF STITCH HOW-TOS

1 Make the initial chain very loose; you will work the puff stitch into it and need space for multiple stitches.

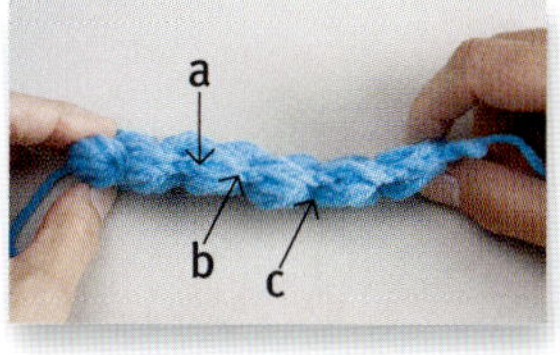

2. a) Head of the puff stitch; b) chain-1 space between the puff stitches; c) side of the puff stitch.

3. Insert hook into side of the stitch from previous row just below the head (see arrow), and complete sc.

4. Work the puff stitch in the chain-1 before (or to the right of) the same puff stitch (see arrow).

5. After working all the yarn overs into the chain-1 space, there are 13 loops on the hook, as shown.

6. At the end, work the last double crochet into the very edge of the piece, as shown.

Convertible Mittens

Lend a hand to cold fingers with pop-top mittens by Donna Childs. The caps are knit separately and sewn to the bases.

KNITTED MEASUREMENTS

Hand circumference 7½"/19cm

SIZE

Sized for Women's Medium.

MATERIALS

2 3½oz/100g hanks (each approx 168yd/154m) of Claudia's Hand Painted Yarns *Worsted Weight* (merino wool) in navy olive (4)

Set of 4 size 7 (4.5mm) double-pointed needles (dpns) OR SIZE TO OBTAIN GAUGE

Stitch markers

Small amount of scrap yarn

GAUGE

22 sts and 30 rnds = 4"/10cm over St st using size 7 (4.5mm) needles.

STITCH GLOSSARY

M1R Insert LH needle from back to front under bar between sts, k through front loop to twist the st.

M1L Insert LH needle from front to back under bar between sts, k through back loop to twist the st.

MITTENS (make 2)

Cast on 42 sts and distribute evenly over 3 dpns. Place marker and join, taking care not to twist sts. Work in k1, p1 rib for 4"/10cm. K 2 rnds.

Next rnd K1, place marker (pm), M1L, k2, M1R, pm, k to end. K 1 rnd.

Next (inc) rnd K1, sl marker, M1L, k to next marker, M1R, sl marker, k to end. Rep inc rnd every other rnd 4 times more—14 sts between markers. K 2 rnds. Rep inc rnd every 3rd rnd twice more—18 sts between markers. K 2 rnds.

Next rnd K to first marker, place 18 sts on scrap yarn, cast on 2 sts, k to end—42 sts. K 10 rnds. Work in k1, p1 rib for 6 rnds. Bind off in rib.

Thumb

Place 18 thumb sts divided evenly over 3 dpns. Attach yarn and k 1 rnd, picking up 2 sts along cast-on sts—20 sts. Place marker. K 10 rnds.

Next (dec) rnd *K2, k2tog; rep from * around—15 sts. K 1 rnd.

Next (dec) rnd *K1, k2tog; rep from * around—10 sts. K 1 rnd.

Next (dec) rnd *K2tog; rep from * around—5 sts. Cut yarn, leaving a long tail. Thread through rem sts and cinch tightly to close.

MITTEN CAP (MAKE 2)

Cast on 42 sts and arrange over 3 dpns as foll: *Needle #1* 21 sts; *Needle #2* 11 sts; *Needle #3* 10 sts. Place marker and join, taking care not to twist sts. P 1 rnd. K 1 rnd. P 1 rnd. K 10 rnds.

Next (dec) rnd *Needle #1* K1, ssk, k to last 3 sts, k2tog, k1; *Needle #2* K1, ssk, k to end; *Needle #3* K to last 3 sts, k2tog, k1—38 sts. Rep dec rnd every other rnd 4 times more—11 sts on Needle #1. Rep dec rnd every rnd 3 times more—5 sts on Needle #1. Place sts from Needle #3 onto Needle #2 (5 sts). Join sts on Needle #1 tog with sts on Needle #2, using 3-needle bind-off (see page 144).

FINISHING

Sew bottom edge of cap to the lowest rnd of ribbing on top of mitten along one side, leaving palm side open. Sew 2nd as for first, making sure opening is on opposite side, so left and right palms are open.✣

Techniques & Abbreviations

Knitting Needles

U.S.	METRIC
0	2mm
1	2.25mm
2	2.75mm
3	3.25mm
4	3.5mm
5	3.75mm
6	4mm
7	4.5mm
8	5mm
9	5.5mm
10	6mm
10½	6.5mm
11	8mm
13	9mm
15	10mm
17	12.75mm
19	15mm
35	19mm

Crochet Hooks

U.S.	METRIC
B/1	2.25mm
C/2	2.75mm
D/3	3.25mm
E/4	3.5mm
F/5	3.75mm
G/6	4mm
7	4.5mm
H/8	5mm
I/9	5.5mm
J/10	6mm
K/10½	6.5mm
L/11	8mm
M/13	9mm
N/15	10mm

Standard Yarn Weight System

Categories of yarn, gauge ranges, and recommended needle and hook sizes

Yarn Weight Symbol & Category Names	0 Lace	1 Super Fine	2 Fine	3 Light	4 Medium	5 Bulky	6 Super Bulky
Type of Yarns in Category	Fingering 10 count crochet thread	Sock, Fingering, Baby	Sport, Baby	DK, Light Worsted	Worsted, Afghan, Aran	Chunky, Craft, Rug	Bulky, Roving
Knit Gauge Range* in Stockinette Stitch to 4 inches	33 –40** sts	27–32 sts	23–26 sts	21–24 sts	16–20 sts	12–15 sts	6–11 sts
Recommended Needle in Metric Size Range	1.5–2.25 mm	2.25–3.25 mm	3.25–3.75 mm	3.75–4.5 mm	4.5–5.5 mm	5.5–8 mm	8 mm and larger
Recommended Needle U.S. Size Range	000 to 1	1 to 3	3 to 5	5 to 7	7 to 9	9 to 11	11 and larger
Crochet Gauge* Ranges in Single Crochet to 4 inch	32-42 double crochets**	21–32 sts	16–20 sts	12–17 sts	11–14 sts	8–11 sts	5–9 sts
Recommended Hook in Metric Size Range	Steel*** 1.6–1.4mm Regular hook 2.25 mm	2.25–3.5 mm	3.5–4.5 mm	4.5–5.5 mm	5.5–6.5 mm	6.5–9 mm	9 mm and larger
Recommended Hook U.S. Size Range	Steel*** 6, 7, 8 Regular hook B–1	B–1 to E–4	E–4 to 7	7 to I–9	I–9 to K–10½	K–10½ to M–13	M–13 and larger

* GUIDELINES ONLY: The above reflect the most commonly used gauges and needle or hook sizes for specific yarn categories.

** Lace weight yarns are usually knitted or crocheted on larger needles and hooks to create lacy, openwork patterns. Accordingly, a gauge range is difficult to determine. Always follow the gauge stated in your pattern.

*** Steel crochet hooks are sized differently from regular hooks--the higher the number, the smaller the hook, which is the reverse of regular hook sizing.

Skill Levels

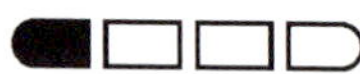

1. **BEGINNER** Ideal first project.

2. **VERY EASY VERY VOGUE** Basic stitches, minimal shaping and simple finishing.

3. **INTERMEDIATE** For knitters with some experience. More intricate stitches, shaping and finishing.

4. **EXPERIENCED** For knitters able to work patterns with complicated shaping and finishing.

Basic Stitches

GARTER STITCH Knit every row. Circular knitting: Knit one round, then purl one round.

STOCKINETTE STITCH Knit right-side rows and purl wrong-side rows. Circular knitting: Knit all rounds. (U.K.: stocking stitch)

REVERSE-STOCKINETTE STITCH Purl right-side rows and knit wrong-side rows. Circular knitting: Purl all rounds. (U.K.: reverse stocking stitch)

Glossary

BIND OFF Used to finish an edge or segment. Lift the first stitch over the second, the second over the third, etc. (U.K.: cast off)

BIND OFF IN RIBBING Work in ribbing as you bind off. (Knit the knit stitches, purl the purl stitches.) (U.K.: cast off in ribbing)

3-NEEDLE BIND-OFF With the right side of the two pieces facing and the needles parallel, insert a third needle into the first stitch on each needle and knit them together. Knit the next two stitches the same way. Slip the first stitch on the third needle over the second stitch and off the needle. Repeat for 3-needle bind-off. (See page 144.)

CAST ON Placing a foundation row of stitches upon the needle in order to begin knitting. (See pages 140–141.)

DECREASE Reduce the stitches in a row (that is, knit 2 together).

INCREASE Add stitches in a row (that is, knit into front and back of stitch).

KNITWISE Insert the needle into the stitch as if you were going to knit it.

MAKE ONE With the needle tip, lift the strand between the last stitch knit and the next stitch on the left-hand needle and knit into back of it. One knit stitch has been added.

MAKE ONE PURL STITCH With the needle tip, lift the strand between the last stitch worked and the next stitch on the left-hand needle and purl it. One purl stitch has been added.

NO STITCH On some charts, "no stitch" is indicated with shaded spaces where stitches have been decreased or not yet made. In such cases, work the stitches of the chart, skipping over the "no stitch" spaces.

PICK UP AND KNIT (PURL) Knit (or purl) into the loops along an edge.

PLACE MARKER Place or attach a loop of contrast yarn or purchased stitch marker as indicated.

PURLWISE Insert the needle into the stitch as if you were going to purl it.

SELVAGE STITCH Edge stitch that helps make seaming easier.

SLIP, SLIP, KNIT Slip next two stitches knitwise, one at a time, to right-hand needle. Insert tip of left-hand needle into fronts of these stitches, from left to right. Knit them together. One stitch has been decreased.

SLIP, SLIP, SLIP, KNIT Slip next three stitches knitwise, one at a time, to right-hand needle. Insert tip of left-hand needle into fronts of these stitches, from left to right. Knit them together. Two stitches have been decreased.

SLIP STITCH An unworked stitch made by passing a stitch from the left-hand to the right-hand needle as if to purl.

WORK EVEN Continue in pattern without increasing or decreasing. (U.K.: work straight)

YARN OVER Making a new stitch by wrapping the yarn over the right-hand needle. (U.K.: yfwd, yon, yrn)

Gauge

Make a test swatch at least 4"/10cm square. If the number of stitches and rows does not correspond to the gauge given, you must change the needle size. An easy rule to follow is: To get fewer stitches to the inch/cm, use a larger needle; to get more stitches to the inch/cm, use a smaller needle. Continue to try different needle sizes until you get the same number of stitches as in the gauge.

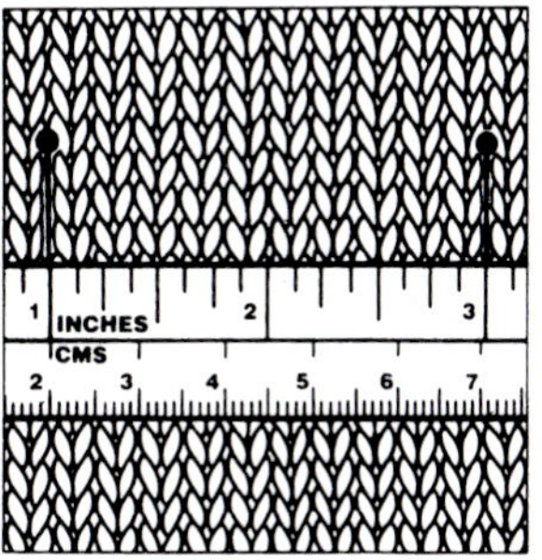

Stitches measured over 2"/5cm.

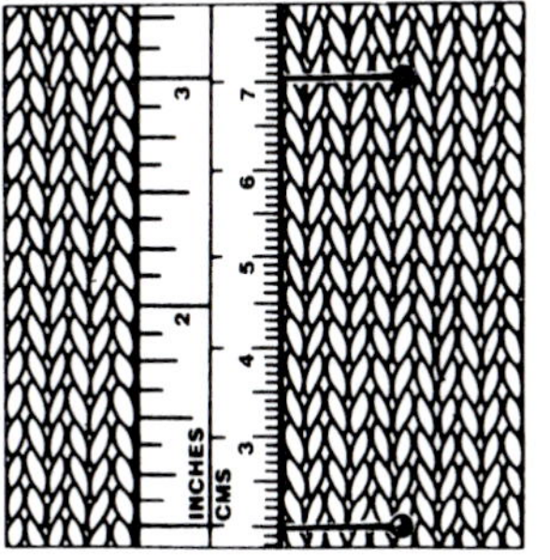

Rows measured over 2"/5cm.

Abbreviations

approx	approximately
beg	begin(ning)
CC	contrasting color
ch	chain
cm	centimeter(s)
cn	cable needle
cont	continu(e)(ing)
dc	double crochet (UK: tr—treble)
dec	decreas(e)(ing)
dpn(s)	double-pointed needle(s)
foll	follow(s)(ing)
g	gram(s)
inc	increas(e)(ing)
k	knit
kfb	knit into the front and back of a stitch—one stitch increased
k2tog	knit 2 stitches together—one stitch has been decreased
LH	left-hand
lp(s)	loop(s)
m	meter(s)
MC	main color
mm	millimeter(s)
M1	make one (see glossary)
M1 p-st	make 1 purl stitch (see glossary)
oz	ounce(s)
p	purl
pat(s)	pattern(s)
pm	place marker (see glossary)
psso	pass slip stitch(es) over
p2tog	purl two stitches together—one stitch decreased
rem	remain(s)(ing)
rep	repeat
RH	right-hand
rnd(s)	round(s)
RS	right side(s)
sc	single crochet (UK: dc—double crochet)
SKP	slip 1, knit 1, pass slip stitch over knit 1—one stitch has been decreased
SK2P	slip 1, knit 2 together, pass slip stitch over the knit 2 together—two stitches decreased
S2KP	slip 2 stitches together, knit 1, pass 2 slip stitches over knit 1—2 stitches decreased
sl	slip
sl st	slip stitch (see glossary)
ssk	slip, slip, knit (see glossary)
sssk	slip, slip, slip, knit (see glossary)
st(s)	stitch(es)
St st	stockinette stitch
tbl	through back loop(s)
tog	together
WS	wrong side(s)
wyib	with yarn in back
wyif	with yarn in front
yd	yard(s)
yo	yarn over needle (see glossary; U.K.: yfwd, yon, yrn)
*	repeat directions following * as many times as indicated
[ ]	repeat directions inside brackets as many times as indicated

Knitting Techniques

SINGLE (LOOP) CAST-ON

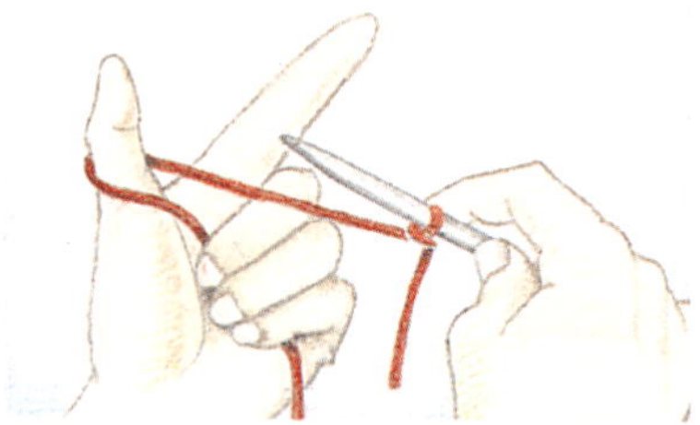

1. Place a slipknot on the right needle, leaving a short tail. Wrap the yarn from the ball around your left thumb from front to back and secure it in your palm with your other fingers.

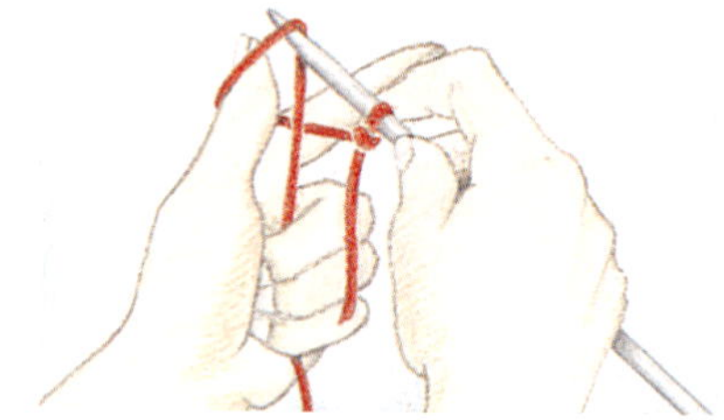

2. Insert the needle upward through the strand on your thumb.

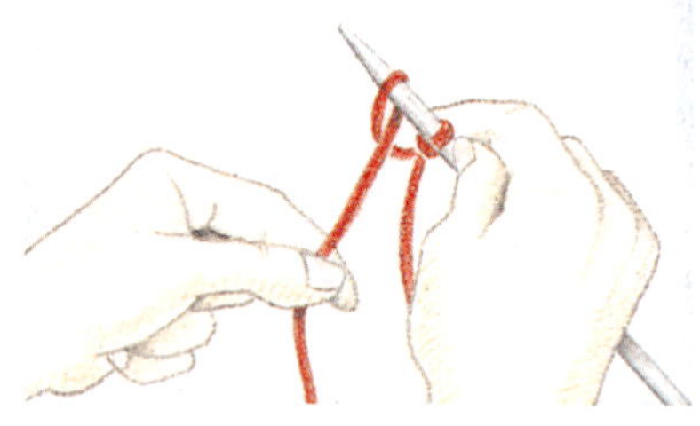

3. Slip this loop from your thumb onto the needle, pulling the yarn from the ball to tighten it. Continue in this way until all the stitches are cast on.

DOUBLE CAST-ON

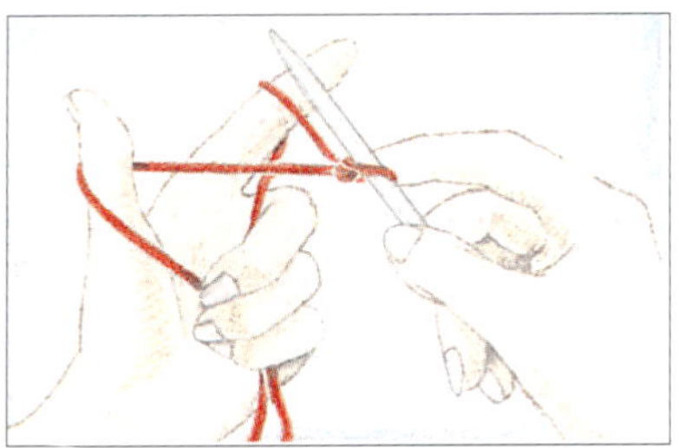

1. Make a slipknot on the right needle, leaving a long tail. Wind the tail end around your left thumb, front to back. Wrap the yarn from the ball over your left index finger and secure the ends in your palm.

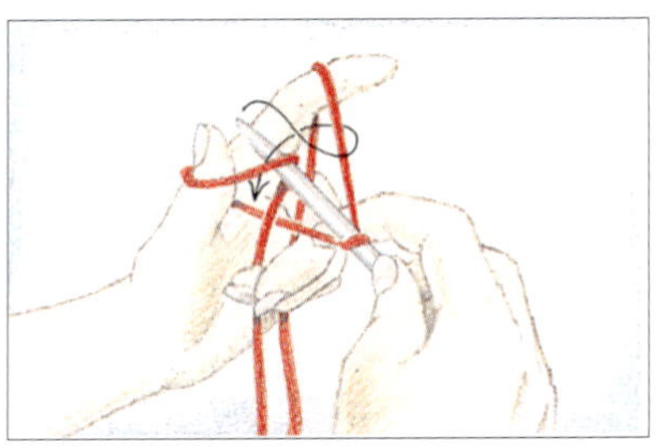

2. Insert the needle upward in the loop on your thumb. Then with the needle, draw the yarn from the ball through the loop to form a stitch.

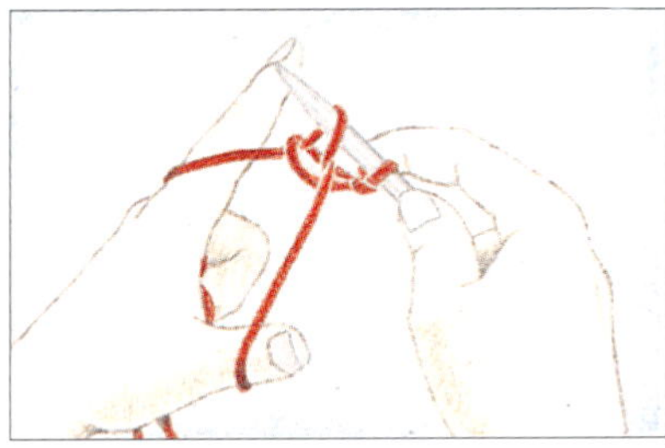

3. Take your thumb out of the loop and tighten the loop on the needle. Continue in this way until all the stitches are cast on.

CABLE CAST-ON

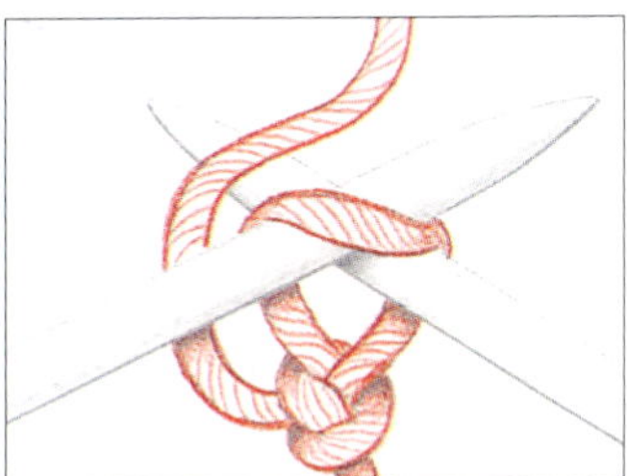

1. Make a slipknot on the left needle. Insert the right needle knitwise into the stitch on the left needle. Wrap the yarn around the right needle as if to knit.

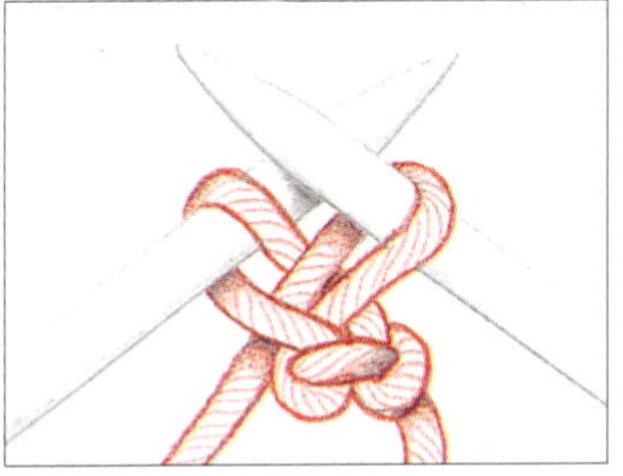

2. Draw the yarn through the first stitch to make a new stitch, but do not drop the stitch from the left needle.

3. Slip the new stitch to the left needle as shown.

4. *Insert the right needle between the two stitches on the left needle.

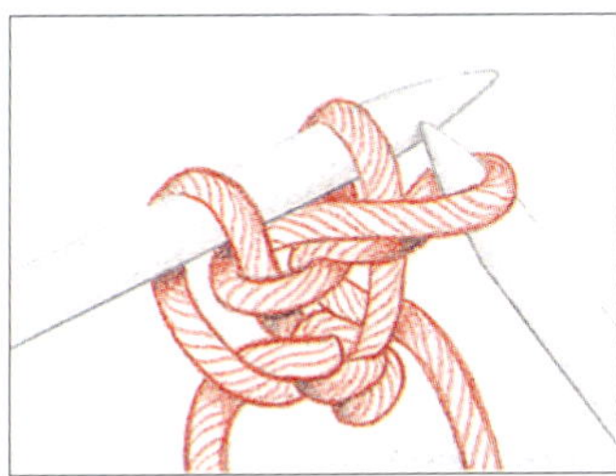

5. Wrap the yarn around the right needle as if to knit and pull the yarn through to make a new stitch.

6. Place the new stitch on the left needle as shown. Repeat from * in step 4, always inserting the right needle in between the last two stitches on the left needle.

CROCHET CHAIN STITCH

1. Make a slipknot near the end of the hook, then wrap the working yarn (the yarn attached to the ball or skein) around the hook as shown. Draw the yarn through the loop on the hook by catching it with the hook and pulling it toward you.

2. One chain stitch is complete. Repeat to create as many chain stitches as required, adding beads between stitches if desired.

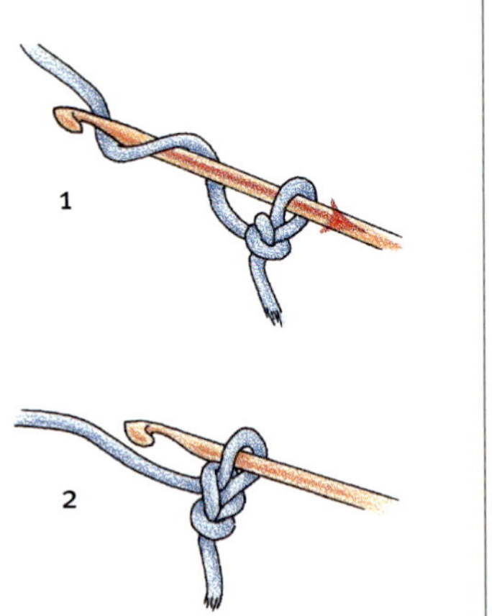

CABLES

Front (or left) cable

1 Slip the first three stitches of the cable purlwise to a cable needle and hold them to the front of the work. Be careful not to twist the stitches.

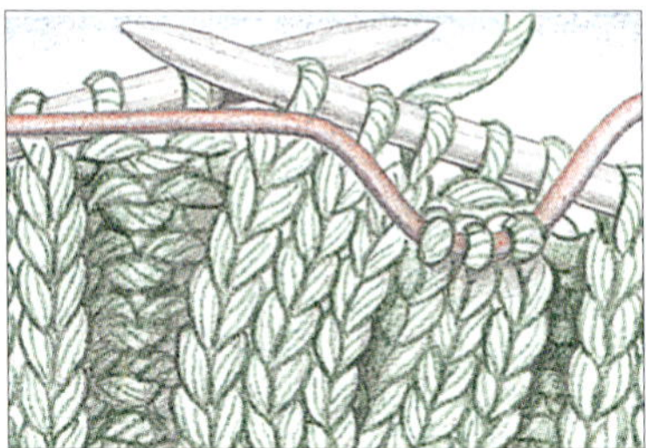

2 Leave the stitches suspended in front of the work, keeping them in the center of the cable needle where they won't slip off. Pull the yarn firmly and knit the next three stitches.

3 Knit the three stitches from the cable needle or return the stitches to the left needle and then knit them.

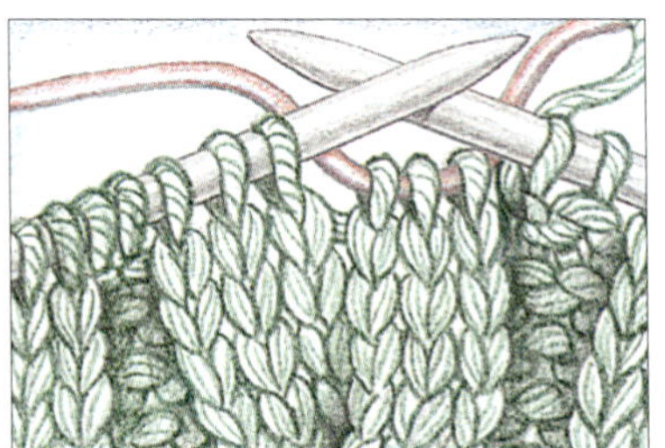

Back (or right) cable

1 Slip the first three stitches of the cable purlwise to a cable needle and hold them to the back of the work. Be careful not to twist the stitches.

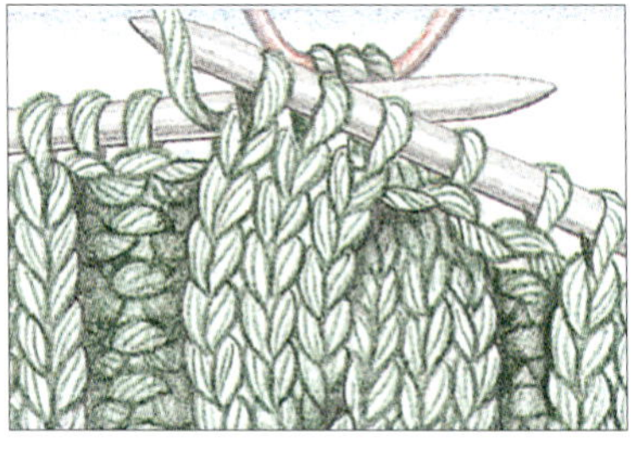

2 Leave the stitches suspended in back of the work, keeping them in the center of the cable needle where they won't slip off. Pull the yarn firmly and knit the next three stitches.

3 Knit the three stitches from the cable needle or return the stitches to the left needle and then knit them.

YARN OVERS There are different ways to make a yarn over. Which method to use depends on where you are in the stitch pattern. If you do not make the yarn over in the right way, you may lose it on the following row, or make a yarn over that is too big. Here are some variations:

Between two knit stitches: Bring the yarn from the back of the work to the front between the two needles. Knit the next stitch, bringing the yarn to the back over the right-hand needle, as shown.

Between a knit and a purl stitch: Bring the yarn from the back to the front between the two needles. Then bring it to the back over the right-hand needle and back to the front again, as shown.
Purl the next stitch.

Between a purl and a knit stitch: Leave the yarn at the front of the work. Knit the next stitch, bringing the yarn to the back over the right-hand needle, as shown.

Between two purl stitches: Leave the yarn at the front of the work. Bring the yarn to the back over the right-hand needle and to the front again, as shown.
Purl the next stitch.

Multiple yarn overs (two or more): Wrap the yarn around the needle, as when working a single yarn over, then continue wrapping the yarn around the needle as many times as indicated. Work the next stitch of the left-hand needle. On the following row, work stitches into the extra yarn overs as described in the pattern. The illustration on the right depicts a finished yarn over on the purl side.

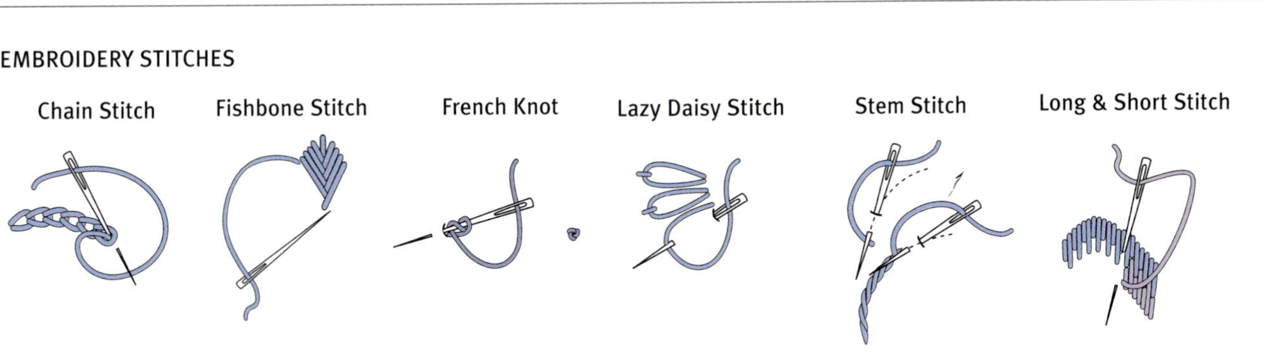

GRAFTING (KITCHENER STITCH)

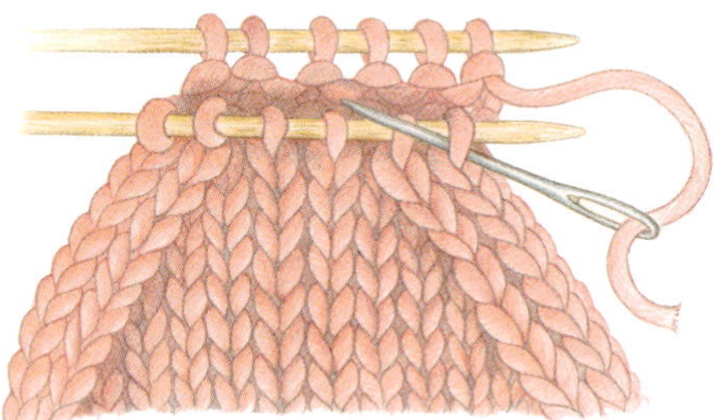

1. Insert tapestry needle purlwise (as shown) through first stitch on front needle. Pull yarn through, leaving that stitch on knitting needle.

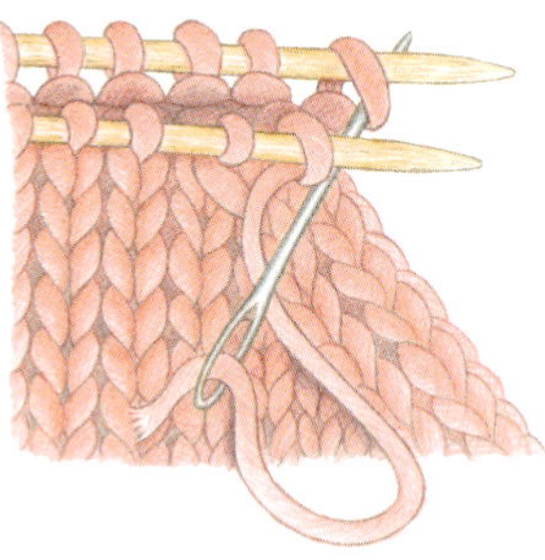

2. Insert tapestry needle knitwise (as shown) through first stitch on back needle. Pull yarn through, leaving stitch on knitting needle.

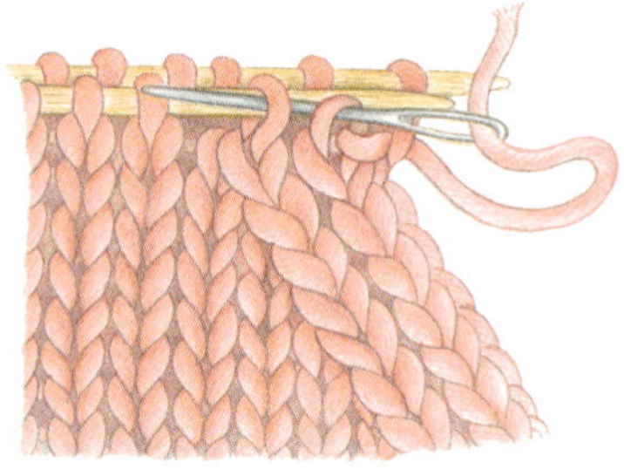

3. Insert tapestry needle knitwise through first stitch on front needle, slip stitch off needle and insert tapestry needle purlwise (as shown) through next stitch on front needle. Pull yarn through, leaving this stitch on needle.

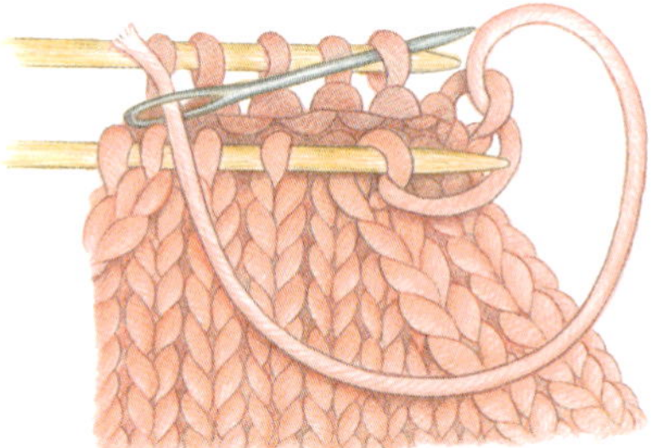

4. Insert tapestry needle purlwise through first stitch on back needle. Slip stitch off needle and insert tapestry needle knitwise (as shown) through next stitch on back needle. Pull yarn through, leaving this stitch on needle.
Repeat steps 3 and 4 until all stitches on both front and back needles have been grafted. Fasten off and weave in end.

3-NEEDLE BIND-OFF This bind-off is used to join two edges that have the same number of stitches, such as shoulder edges, which have been placed on holders.

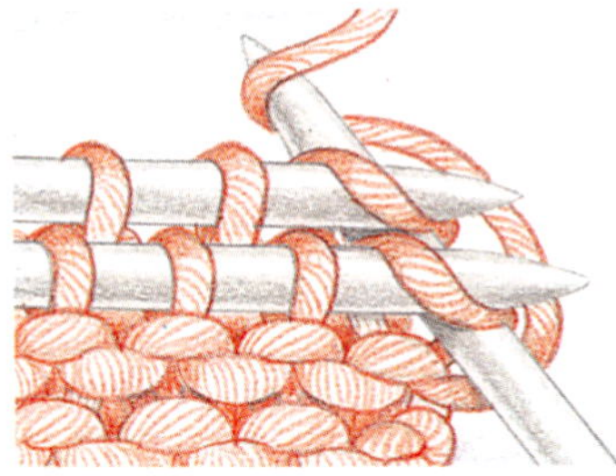

1. With the right side of the two pieces facing each other, and the needles parallel, insert a third needle knitwise into the first stitch of each needle. Wrap the yarn around the needle as if to knit.

2. Knit these two stitches together and slip them off the needles. *Knit the next two stitches together in the same way as shown.

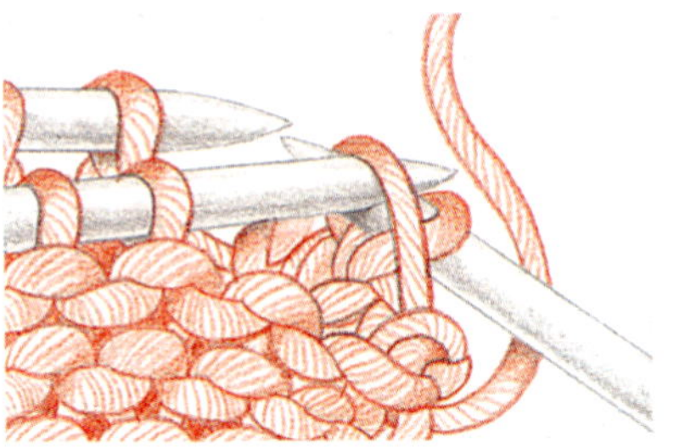

3. Slip the first stitch on the third needle over the second stitch and off the needle. Repeat from the * in step 2 across the row until all the stitches are bound off.

TASSELS

Cut a piece of cardboard to the desired length of the tassel. Wrap yarn around the cardboard. Knot a piece of yarn tightly around one end, cut as shown, and remove the cardboard. Wrap and tie yarn around the tassel about 1"/2.5cm down from the top to secure the fringe.

I-CORD

Cast on about three to five sitches. *Knit one row. Without turning the work, slip the stitches back to the beginning of the row. Pull the yarn tightly from the end of the row. Repeat from the * as desired. Bind off.

POM-POMS

1. With two circular pieces of cardboard the width of the desired pom-pom, cut a center hole. Then cut a pie-shaded wedge out of the circle.

2. Hold the two circles together and wrap the yarn around the cardboard. Carefully cut around the cardboard.

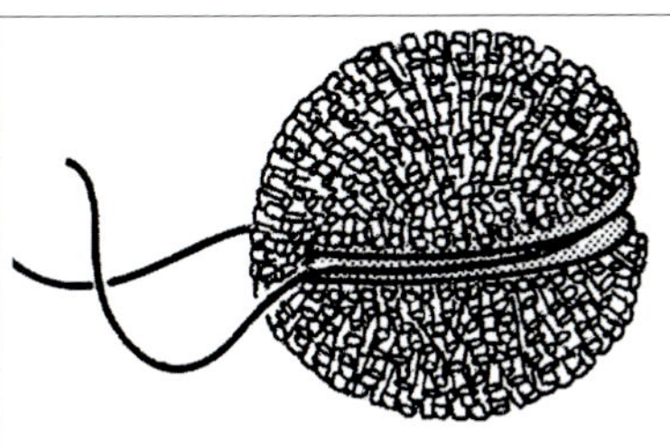

3. Tie a piece of yarn tightly between the two circles. Remove the cardboard.

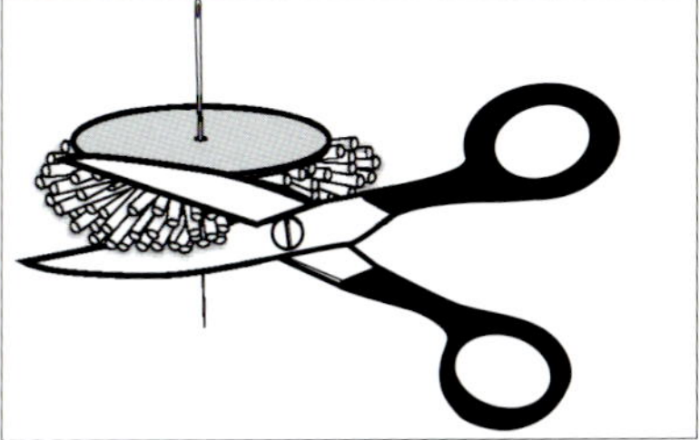

4. Sandwich pom-pom between two round pieces of cardboard held together with a long needle. Cut around circumference for a perfect pom-pom.

DUPLICATE STITCH

Duplicate stitch covers a knit stitch. Bring the needle up below the stitch to be worked. Insert the needle under both loops one row above and pull it through. Insert it back into the stitch below and through the center of the next stitch in one motion, as shown.

Resources

Alchemy Yarns of Transformation
P.O. Box 1080
Sebastopol, CA 95473
www.alchemyyarns.com

Alpaca With a Twist
950 S. White River Parkway West Dr.
Indianapolis, IN 46221
www.alpacawithatwist.com

Artyarns
39 Westmoreland Avenue
White Plains, NY 10606
www.artyarns.com

AslanTrends
8 Maple Street
Port Washington, NY 11050
www.aslantrends.com

Classic Elite Yarns
122 Western Avenue
Lowell, MA 01851
www.classiceliteyarns.com

Claudia Hand Painted Yarns
40 West Washington Street
Harrisonburg, VA 22802
www.claudiaco.com

Dale of Norway
4750 Shelburne Road, Suite 20
Shelburne, VT 05482
www.dale.no/us/

Debbie Bliss
Distributed by KFI
www.debbieblissonline.com

Fairmount Fibers, Ltd.
915 North 28th Street
Philadelphia, PA 19130
www.fairmountfibers.com

Fiesta Yarns
5401 San Diego Avenue NE
Albuquerque, NM 87113
www.fiestayarns.com

Jade Sapphire Exotic Fibres
www.jadesapphire.com

Jamieson's of Shetland
Distributed by Simply Shetland
www.jamiesonsshetland.co.uk

JCA, Inc.
35 Scales Lane
Townsend, MA 01469
www.jcacrafts.com

KFI
P.O. Box 336
315 Bayview Avenue
Amityville, NY 11701
www.knittingfever.com

Knit One, Crochet Too, Inc.
91 Tandberg Trail, Unit 6
Windham, ME 04062
www.knitonecrochettoo.com

Koigu Wool Designs
P.O. Box 158
Chatsworth, ON N0H 1G0
Canada
www.koigu.com

Lana Grossa
Distributed by Muench Yarns
www.lanagrossa.com

Lion Brand Yarn Co.
34 West 15th Street
New York, NY 10011
www.lionbrand.com

Lorna's Laces
4229 North Honore Street
Chicago, IL 60613
www.lornaslaces.net

Louet North America
808 Commerce Park Drive
Ogdensburg, NY 13669
www.louet.com

Manos del Uruguay
Distributed by Fairmount Fibers, Ltd.
www.manos.com.uy

Muench Yarns
1323 Scott Street
Petaluma, CA 94954
www.muenchyarns.com

Nashua Handknits
Distributed by Westminster Fibers, Inc.

Reynolds
Distributed by JCA, Inc.

Skacel Collection, Inc.
P.O. Box 88110
Seattle, WA 98138
www.skacelknitting.com

Simply Shetland
18375 Olympic Avenue South
Seattle, WA 98188
www.simplyshetland.net

Westminster Fibers, Inc.
165 Ledge Street
Nashua, NH 03060
www.westminsterfibers.com

Zitron
Distributed by Skacel Collection, Inc.

Index